Tom Zimmerman

2008

PARADISE
PROMOTED

ACP

ANGEL CITY PRESS

LOS ANGELES:

A CITY WHERE . . .

ALL the MEN RETAINED THEIR VIGOR...

ALL THE WOMEN WERE BEAUTY QUEENS . . .

EVERYBODY TOOK PICTURES...

HOLLYWOOD STARS
EXERCISED RIGHT BY THEIR BUNGALOWS . . .

AND EVEN THE OIL FIELDS HAD PALM TREES . . .

AND WHERE ABSOLUTELY EVERYBODY
HAD HIS OWN CAR.

St. Peter: DO YOU SEEK ENTRANCE HERE?

Californian: QUITE THE REVERSE, BROTHER! WE'VE COME TO SEE IF WE CAN SELL
YOU ON LOS ANGELES.

1925

In Los Angeles

It's fun to be a tourist
And with the tourists stand,
A happy smile upon your face,
A guide-book in your hand;
A yellow poppy on your breast,
Orange blossoms in your hair,
Ramona handy in your grip,
Time-tables everywhere

It's fun to be a tourist
To climb these mountain walls,
To visit countless canyons
With streams and waterfalls;
To see them all, then gaily
Down to the beach to trip,
And in the old Pacific
Take your initial dip.

It's fun to be a tourist,
Your first orange grove to see,
To eat your first ripe olive
Fresh picked from off the tree;
To gaze upon the date-palms,
And eucalyptus trees,
And at the graceful peppers
Slow swaying in the breeze.

It's fun to be a tourist,
An ostrich farm to view,
To see the ancient missions
And modern oil wells, too
To buy a bunch of post cards,
A thousand at the least,
To send to friends of old lang syne,
Who still are in the East.

Copyright June, 1913, by H.C. Hurst

HAVEN CHARLES HURST

1913

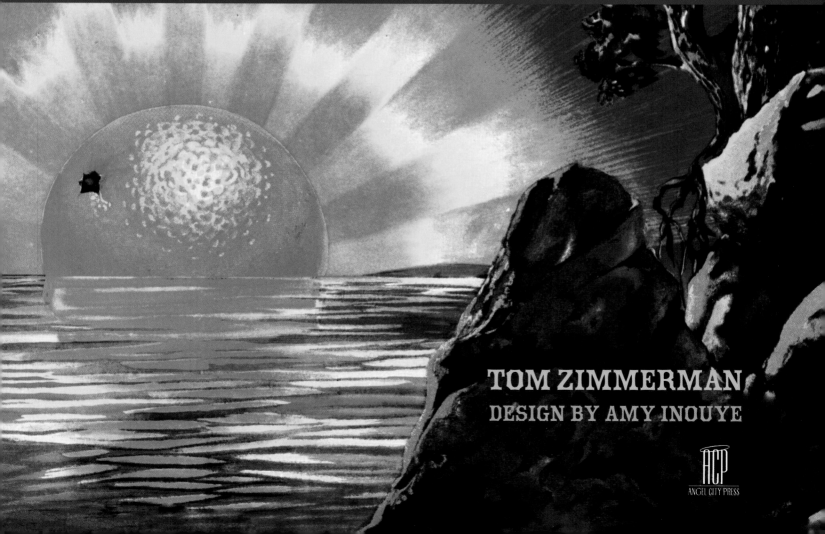

PARADISE PROMOTED

THE BOOSTER CAMPAIGN THAT CREATED LOS ANGELES 1870–1930

TOM ZIMMERMAN

DESIGN BY AMY INOUYE

ACP

ANGEL CITY PRESS

Paradise Promoted
The Booster Campaign that Created Los Angeles
Copyright © 2008 by Tom Zimmerman

Designed by Amy Inouye • futurestudio.com

10 9 8 7 6 5 4 3 2 1

ISBN-13 978-1-883318-64-2

LIBRARY OF CONGRESS CATALOGING-IN-PUBLICATION DATA

Zimmerman, Tom.
 Paradise promoted : the booster campaign that created Los Angeles, 1870–1930 / by Tom Zimmerman ; design by Amy Inouye.
   p. cm.
 Summary: "With more than 500 photographs and rare ephemera, all collected by author Tom Zimmerman, Paradise promoted is the first book to showcase the era from 1870 to 1930 when boosters developed the small town of Los Angeles into the city that would become Americas most cutting-edge metropolis"— Provided by publisher.
 Includes bibliographical references and index.
 ISBN 978-1-883318-64-2 (hardcover : alk. paper)
 1. City promotion—California—Los Angeles—History—19th century.
 2. City promotion—California—Los Angeles—History—20th century.
 3. Los Angeles (Calif.)—Economic conditions—19th century. 4. Los Angeles (Calif.)—Economic conditions--20th century. 5. Los Angeles (Calif.)—History—Pictorial works. 6. Los Angeles (Calif.)—History—Sources. 7. City promotion—United States—Case studies. 8. Cities and towns—United States—Growth—Case studies. I. Title.

HT325.Z56 2008
979.4'9404–dc22

                    2007044790

Printed in China

ANGEL CITY PRESS

2118 Wilshire Blvd. #880
Santa Monica, California 90403
310.395.9982
www.angelcitypress.com

In an effort to make their section stand out, the boosters always capitalized "Southern California." As Charles Lummis pointed out, it was "a popular but not a political entity." To allow the promoters to rest comfortably in their graves, the practice will be continued here.

Preceding pages:

Page 4: Hundred-year-old man skipping rope. c. 1925

Page 5: Miss Los Angeles beauty contest. c. 1939

Page 6: Tourist photo marked "Jane, Los Angeles, 1916."

Page 7: Shirley Mason, actress sister of Viola Dana, exercises. c. 1924

Page 8: A scenic Los Angeles oil field. c. 1924

Page 9: Al Barnes' Zoo, Culver City. March 22, 1926

My father's first place in Sunny SoCal was a duplex on Bay Street in Santa Monica near the Douglas plant.

DEDICATION

*To my father, Pius Zimmerman, who came to Los Angeles from North Dakota in 1933
because he loved airplanes and hated farming.
And to my mother, Catherine Colette Albrecht, who didn't run away at age five
when her parents told her they were leaving Chicago for Los Angeles in 1925.*

My mother and her parents lived on the second floor of a duplex in Highland Park on Avenue 55. Out front is the Buick that brought the family to L.A. from Chicago.

Advantages of Los Angeles

Speech delivered by Clinton E. Miller, representing the Los Angeles Realty Board, before the Annual Convention of the National Association of Real Estate Exchanges in St. Louis, Missouri, on June 19, 1918. He won a national competition for best five-minute speech on advantages of the speaker's home city. Mr. Miller brought home a silver loving cup from the Chicago Real Estate Board. Miller's speech is reprinted with spelling and grammar intact.

In preparation for the building of the city I shall describe out there in Southern California, Nature did her best. She first laid down a fertile valley and back of it to the north and east she piled a semicircle of mighty mountain peaks to protect it from the extremes of climate of the Great Central Plain; upon those magnificent summits she stored the everlasting snows that feed the irrigating canals; at the western border of this valley she placed the great Pacific Ocean—the sea of commercial supremacy of the future. To finish the arrangements properly she caused a great stream of warm water—the Japan current—to flow near the shore so that there is never a day but the blossoms blow and the mocking bird sings always.

At the higher altitudes of these protecting mountains are great forests of timber surrounding lakes filled with trout; underneath the lower slopes where the trees do not grow and the land is too rough for agriculture are subterranean lakes full of crude oil, the development of which has placed this region first in the United States in oil exports.

Add to these natural advantages a climate with a mean annual temperature of 62.8 degrees and the stage is certainly set for the production of a masterpiece in the building of a city.

And that has been accomplished because in the heart of it all California builded her most famous city and called it Los Angeles—"the City of the Angels"—which in the beginning was a Spanish pueblo, but now is a metropolitan city of over a half million that is well and artistically lighted, properly paved, sewered, watered, policed and governed.

Beginning in 1870 this city has doubled its population every ten years and present indications assure the soundness of President Garland's slogan, "A Million in 1920." These are very significant facts, gentlemen. Boastful advertising may bring people to a city, but it required something else to make them stay.

And what has made them stay in Los Angeles? First, schools—always first in America—the training camps for citizenship, and no city is greater than the quality of its citizenship. Los Angeles pays more per capita for public education than any other city in the United States. In eight hundred school buildings, eighty-three thousand children are trained by over three thousand teachers—the best-paid and best-trained corps in the world.

Our county leads the United States in agricultural and horticultural production. It has the finest system of concrete asphalt boulevards, upon which, from the mountains to the

Foster and Kleiser was in the billboard business, but played its part in the promotional campaign as did so many other Southland companies. Real-estate and department-store ads were staples. The swimwear featured in the J.W. Robinson Company ad was part of a major L.A. industry. Los Angeles was dominant in democratic, comfortable casual clothing.

Top: Dickinson and Gillespie bought land all over the United States to subdivide. The company moved its offices to Los Angeles in 1924 and bought Palisades del Rey in the emptiness of the far western section of the city, working with Harry Culver to develop the area. They had noted the effect higher education had on Palo Alto with Stanford and Westwood with UCLA, so in 1927 Culver donated one hundred acres to the Jesuits to build a new campus for their Loyola College on the bluff in what is now Westchester. Today, as Loyola Marymount University, it is the direct descendant of L.A.'s first college, St. Vincent's, which started in 1895.

Opposite, top to bottom: Couple in G. H. Lovewell's California Studio on N. Spring Street with an "orange tree." c. 1929; Postcard view of the Ocean Park Bath House. 1912; Visiting Eagle Rock; On the road to Anaheim, having seen *It Happened One Night.* Note that the signs are all produced by the Auto Club; On the summit of Mount Grayback, the highest point in San Bernardino County at 11,502 feet. It's officially called Mount San Gorgonio. November 14, 1932

Hand-colored souvenir postcard of a young lady in a fine dress at the Orange Studio, 520 S. Broadway. 1912

Opposite, center: Isaias Hellman started the Farmers and Merchants Bank in 1871 and was instrumental in keeping L.A. solvent after the bust of the Boom of the '80s. His brother Herman eventually joined him at the bank. Herman's sons Marco and Irving started the Hellman Bank in 1913. One of their first acquisitions was the straightforwardly named All Night and Day Bank.

Opposite, far right, top to bottom: Pershing Square (aka Central Park, Sixth Street Park, etc.) is second only to the Plaza as L.A.'s oldest park. The fountain was part of John Parkinson's 1910 redevelopment and took the place of a bandstand. The park was named for World War I commander John J. Pershing; Souvenir postcard in the "orange groves" from Pasadena's Flag Studio subtly thumbs the sender's nose at the folks in the snow zone. c. 1910; Double-exposed tourist photo at an orange stand, February 25, 1923; Henry Knowles, his family and his bear in the Oak Knoll district of Pasadena; She's got to be somebody's baby. Avalon.

sea, roll more automobiles per capita than in any other county. There is an unexcelled electric urban and interurban streetcar system extending to points sixty miles distant.

We are over a billion-dollar city in both bank clearings and property values. Our thirty-two banks cleared over a billion and a half last year.

Time will permit me merely to mention our seventy-five-million-dollar annual citrus crop; our great public library with its twelve branches and twenty-four sub-branches; our wonderful hotels accommodating one hundred fifty thousand people; twenty-five public parks totaling forty-one hundred acres; museums and art galleries; playgrounds and public baths. With all that, Los Angeles' debt per capita is half that of New York City!

While primarily famed as a residence district, because our city has more home owners per capita than any other in the world, yet our industrial and commercial activity is unusual, because over two thousand manufacturing establishments made one hundred fifty million dollars' worth of goods last year. Over two hundred different lines of manufacture are needed now in Los Angeles that will pay profits immediately—a cotton mill, for instance, to use the ten million dollars' worth of Sea Island cotton now growing in Imperial Valley.

And the conditions for manufacture are ideal. From the glaciers of the Sierras two hundred fifty miles away, Los Angeles has led down a mountain stream to the door of every home at a cost of twenty-three million dollars. In its drop this stream generates two hundred fifty thousand horsepower of electric energy to light our homes and boulevards and to run our factories. We annexed a part of the Pacific Ocean and made a ten-million-dollar harbor just the way we wanted it. Here the eighty-million-dollar shipbuilding program is making a record because labor performs twenty-four hours every day in the year.

For these reasons we are a happy, prosperous people whose latchstring is always out. The only quarrel we have among ourselves is whether Los Angeles has a finer climate in winter or in summer. Come out and help us settle the question. There's room for a million more on the tops of our hills, another on their slopes and a third on the plain below. We already have in reserve the economic resources for that growth. Because Christopher Columbus landed on the wrong side of North America, don't perpetuate that error by remaining there all your lives. We need your experience and energy; you need our delightful climate to ease your journey down the western slope of life.

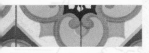

Frank Wiggins, the greatest apostle of Los Angeles, came to the city with death clinging possessively to his coattails. What Peter Clark MacFarlane in *Collier's* magazine called the "resurrectionary climate" of L.A. restored Wiggins to health. He became the secretary of the Chamber of Commerce and spent the next quarter-century devising ways to convince fellow Americans to come out and see the city that saved him. 1895

Yours Truly

Frank Wiggins

CONTENTS

The All Year
Club opened in
1921 to encour-
age twelve-
month tourism
in the South-
land. The group
published pam-
phlets as well as
maps, and she
wears them well.

INTRODUCTION

For sixty years, Los Angeles was the subject of the longest, loudest, most persistent promotional campaign in the history of the United States. Nothing was too exaggerated, absurd or flat-out bizarre to be fodder for the relentless effort to convince Americans to slam the door forever on their home, wherever it was, and move to what booster supreme and *Los Angeles Times* editor G.W. Burton called, "The fairest daughter among the sisterhood of cities in the world."

Paradise Promoted is not a history of Los Angeles. Rather it relates how the city was promoted, largely to other Americans, as an accessible dream, *the* accessible dream. All the hustling started with the railroads trying to sell off the land they had been granted in the splendid isolation of Southern California by federal and local governments in the 1870s. It ended when the Great Depression made it not just undesirable to lure the rest of an impoverished country to Los Angeles, but an economic impossibility.

Access was a problem from the beginning. Los Angeles was far from the population centers of Mexico and the United States. By wagon or ship, the trip was arduous and took months. In addition to its isolation from these population centers, absolutely none of the traditional reasons a city would grow applied to Los Angeles. There was no natural harbor like the one that made San Francisco so accessible, no navigable river like that which opened Sacramento and the interior of the state. It clearly was not located at a natural crossroads; the mountains to the east and north saw to that. All Los Angeles boasted was a reliable water source in the *Río Porciúncula* in both its above- and below-ground manifestations, and what even a skeptic like *Atlantic Monthly* writer Sarah Comstock would admit was "a climate of almost unadulterated delight." But so what? Not only was Los Angeles remote from the rest of the United States, most Americans had never even heard of the place.

All that changed when the city was connected to the transcontinental railroad in 1876. Suddenly, L.A., "Queen of the Cow Counties," was accessible. When the Santa Fe brought in a second transcontinental line in 1886, the trip was not only fairly easy, it was even affordable.

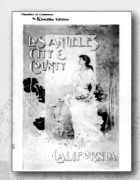

Los Angeles City and County 1897, 1915 and 1921 editions. This was the longest-running of the Chamber of Commerce pamphlets. The illustrated booklet was aimed at introducing Los Angeles and its surrounding towns to prospective citizens. There were articles on climate, the Chamber of Commerce exhibits, agriculture and eventually industry. The 1897 edition was printed specifically to be sent to the miners in the Klondike gold-strike region.

Competition: the wellspring of capitalism. Both the Santa Fe and the Southern Pacific were land-rich due to the subsidies given them to build their lines. Both needed people to ride their trains, settle on their lands and use their freight cars to transfer goods around the country. So they advertised. Suddenly the neglected southern part of California was being loudly and persistently hawked as "Our Italy," "The New Beulah Land" and the home of "Sunlit Skies of Glory."

At first, the efforts were quite staid and directed toward tourists and farmers. Then the second Los Angeles Chamber of Commerce got into the act. Following its inception in 1888, the Chamber rapidly became the largest organization of its kind in the United States. It developed into the entity that coalesced all the efforts to expand both the population and economic base of the city. Social critic Louis Adamic lampooned the endless regional boosterism, but he had to give the Chamber its due, noting that its leadership was "possessed by a mad and powerful drive [to make] this great region of eternal spring sooner or later become the biggest city in the country."

Over the next thirty years promoters got properly warmed up to the task. In the 1920s with funding from the Los Angeles County Board of Supervisors, the All Year Club, the Realty Board, Automobile Club and Sunkist, the Merchants and Manufacturers Association and the Chamber of Commerce let out all stops to induce the rest of the country to relocate to the "Land of Eternal Spring"—also known as "The Home of Contented Labor," "Where Nature Helps Industry Most," "The Metropolis of the Southwest," "The Largest City in the Western Americas," "The Progressive City of the Twentieth Century," "The Wonder City of the United States" and, of course, "Climatic Capital of the New World."

This love of superlative may have started with the professional boosters, but it soon filtered down to the citizenry. San Francisco's boosters were always envious that the everyday man-on-the-street in Los Angeles would eagerly tell anyone who would listen that he lives in the greatest city in history, and that only the severely demented would ever leave it. In 1925, critic Paul Jordan-Smith noted this tendency for locals to think positively. "It became a crime to criticize Southern California; a felony to whisper of an earthquake; to frown upon the climate was equivalent to committing rape."

This expectation of grandiosity had spread all over the country by the 1920s. In 1923, the Religious of the Sacred Heart of Mary, an order of Catholic nuns, had been asked by Archbishop John Cantwell to come to Los Angeles to open a school for girls to be called Marymount-in-the-West. The nuns, who were all Irish, arrived on the Santa Fe railroad from their mother house in Tarrytown, New York. The Sister keeping the *Annals* was a little disappointed upon arriving at the

Los Angeles County California

Boosting the land and creating a romantic past: Christine Sterling described Olvera Street as "forsaken and forgotten . . . suffocated in a cheap, sordid atmosphere" when she first encountered it in 1926. She convinced the Chamber of Commerce and Harry Chandler to help her save and restore this most historic part of Los Angeles. She succeeded, and Olvera Street opened in 1930 as an homage to what she called "the birthplace of the City and . . . the fulfillment of a true Pan-American Ideal."

Top: The original look of what was then largely a Chamber of Commerce promotional publication, *The Land of Sunshine.* 1894

Left: Chamber of Commerce pamphlet on the attractions and industry of Southern California. 1935

Sunkist's original ad ran in the *Des Moines Register* on March 2, 1908. The oranges were delivered in specially marked Southern Pacific trains and the railroad paid for billboards all over Iowa with the legend "Oranges for Health, California for Wealth." Sales went up more than fifty percent in the state. Sunkist was active throughout the rest of the booster campaign, promoting its citrus fruit and products and, by proxy, the Southland that spawned them.

GREET 'EM WITH ORANGES
JAN. 30 - 1926

La Grande Station. She "made mental note that there were no orange groves in sight, and chuckled remembering the tales heard about leaning out the window to pick your own breakfast."

Anyone who flies into Los Angeles at night, or tries to drive around in the city during the day, can see the boosters' success. There are two primary reasons this convoluted campaign worked so well. First, there was something to sell. It is virtually impossible to exaggerate the climate of Southern California. Through a wonderful happenstance of a warm-water current offshore and protective chains of mountains to the colder north and hotter east, the area offers the chance to go to the beach or snow ski on the same day. It is rarely humid, almost never freezes on the coastal plain, and—except for those pesky earthquakes and fires that occasionally rage with a vengeance— is almost never subject to natural disasters that regularly devastate other parts of the country.

The second necessary ingredient was a group of leaders who saw Los Angeles as one huge hunk of clay, ripe for molding. They had a vision of L.A. as one of America's leading cities and dedicated themselves to moving heaven and earth to make this a reality. The climate was natural, but everything else had to be created. They were focused like men possessed with the idea of growth, and boosterism was their means to that end. For Los Angeles to become the Major City these leaders so desperately wanted, its landscape would have to be altered to a degree unprecedented in American history. This business-oriented model was hardly the only vision for the future of Los Angeles. There was a very strong Socialist movement in the early twentieth century, and a concurrent group of artists who saw the Southland as the Modernist capital of America. But none of them had the power, longevity, popularity or the pure booster energy to steer the developing city on that course.

ELEMENTS OF GROWTH

These photographs illustrate two of the necessary ingredients in the unprecedented growth of Los Angeles. The first depicts the construction of the Hollywood Bowl in 1926. It was taken by Eyre Powell for the Wide World photo agency. Within the year, he would be running his own news photography agency for the Chamber of Commerce. It is pretty clear why he fit in so well with them. Instead of wasting his time climbing up the hill to shoot the working men actually grading the earth and laying in the seats, he was down at the bottom snapping away at the "Girls Auxiliary Corps of the Hollywood Studio Club" as they labored mightily with a bunch of boards. Had this been done for the Chamber instead of Wide World, the caption would have pointed out that there was no way to tell if the Girls Auxiliary Corps was working in June or January.

Although it is possible they were actually there to do some carpentry, it's not very likely. Hollywood was constantly trying to find ways to advertise its ingenues, and this appears to be one of them. It is typical of the

S.H. Woodruff

Hollywood's "Girls Auxiliary" starlets help build Hollywood Bowl.

campaign that it was never enough to just illustrate something in Los Angeles. It had to look special, to look amazing, to look like no other place in the country. Pretty girls were an integral part of the equation, so why use one when you can use five? Using beautiful women to promote everything under the sun was not invented in Los Angeles, but it was perfected here. Thanks to Hollywood and the endless supply of beautiful hopefuls flocking to the city from every corner of the Western world to get into the movies, there was never a shortage of models for the promotional campaign.

The second photo, above, shows S.H. Woodruff, the steely-eyed, no-nonsense developer of Hollywoodland, Dana Point and Lakewood. However glowing, healthy, and lush the campaign illustrations were, it took grizzled types like Woodruff to make the dream pay—he was the field general. In Hollywoodland, Pacific Electric Railroad Director, M.H. Sherman and *Los Angeles Times* publisher Harry Chandler merely owned the land and paid the bills. It was up to Woodruff to move the merchandise.

Santa Monica Canyon.
September 9, 1917

Los Angeles was the only one of the various Southern California cities that had both the physical dimensions and aggressive leadership necessary to pull off rapid expansion. Those in power in Los Angeles saw growth as the best way to achieve prosperity. They built a city of newcomers who were as thrilled with the idea of making L.A. the greatest of American cities as they were. The Chamber not only encouraged its secretary, Frank Wiggins, to dream up endless ways to advertise the city, it also established an Agricultural Bureau (and later an Industrial Bureau) so newcomers would have someplace to work.

Top left: One of the many tent cities for tourists, taken with George Eastman's original amateur Kodak camera. c. 1890.

Bottom left: Family in a real orange grove this time. 1905

Below: Venice board-walk. 1911

This is the much-less-discussed aspect of the promotional campaign. The Chamber of Commerce was not simply content to lure people to Los Angeles. They were determined to provide a functioning city in which to live and, most importantly, to provide jobs. The Chamber not only published booster pamphlets by the hundreds of thousands, it also led in the fight for a harbor, water and power sources, gave instruction in proper farming methods for semi-arid, irrigation-dependent land, and lured established industrial concerns to the Southland. As the Chamber's secretary and general manager A.G. Arnall pointed out in 1929, "If we are to maintain our ever-increasing population, we must find work for the newcomers to do, and it is only on the basis of the great industrial structure that a city can be built." With that idea came the expansion of new industries and new dreams. . . .

The ballyhoo ended with the Great Depression and the consequent reluctance to lure even more of the jobless to Los Angeles.

It had been quite a campaign, unique in American history. An irrelevant cowtown like hundreds of others in the West, with no reason at all to become a major city, was transformed in forty years to the fifth-largest city in America, with an industrial base that would significantly aid in the defeat of the Axis enemy in World War II, the busiest harbor on the West Coast and the home of the American entertainment and aviation industries. It would also be the butt of countless jokes due to the excesses of the campaign. People may have chortled, but that didn't keep them from moving to Los Angeles.

CHAPTER ONE

Postcard of Mission San Gabriel, left, and half of a stereo card of the Plaza Church. In 1912 the bell tower of the Church was replaced with a bell wall to make it resemble the mission. The title on the stereo card was "Mission Church." The promoters were always trying to create a romantic past.

MISSION SAN GABRIEL AND PLAZA CHURCH

Mission San Gabriel and the Plaza Church are the two most historic structures in the Los Angeles area. The mission established the first European presence in 1771 (the present church was completed in 1794) and spelled the end of the Gabrieleño/Tongva tribe's dominance of the Southland. The Plaza Church, with all its additions and replacements, has been in continuous use since 1822. That they are both Catholic structures attests to the key role played by the Church in developing the Spanish empire in America.

Tourist photo of the barracks buildings for Companies F and E and the main street through the National Soldiers' Home at Sawtelle, looking north. The home was one of the few national institutions in the fledgling city and was always featured in the early promotional literature. 1909

NATIONAL SOLDIERS' HOME AT SAWTELLE

Harris Newmark noted regarding Los Angeles and the Civil War, "We were so far from the scene of strife that we were not materially affected." The major L.A. contribution to the Union effort came long after Appomattox, in the form of the National Home for Disabled Volunteer Soldiers in Sawtelle for the veterans of that conflict. Initial authorization for such homes came in 1866. In 1877 Congress passed an act to establish a branch in California. The Los Angeles Board of Trade lobbied successfully to have it placed in the Southland. Six hundred acres were donated by Senator John Jones and Arcadia Bandini Stearns de Baker near the nascent town of Sawtelle. The first barracks were completed in 1888 and, over the next century and a quarter, the veterans' center would evolve to aid America's former servicemen.

... **Southern California, a region almost unknown, and just now opened to settlement by the completion of several lines of railroad; and which, by reason of its fine healthful climate, its rich soil, and its remarkably varied products, deserves the attention of farmers looking for pleasant homes and cheap and fertile lands, combined with a climate the best, probably, in the United States.** Charles Nordhoff, *California: A Book for Travelers and Settlers* (1873)

"The Discovery of San Francisco Harbor by Don Gaspar de Portolà," as portrayed by the actors of *The Mission Play.* The Act 1 dialog to accompany the action was, "Next day, accompanied by the whole expedition, I climbed a brown hill and looked down upon that mighty harbor. Not in Spain, Father President, nor anywhere a ship has ever sailed, is there a port to rival the port which we that morning beheld with our wondering eyes."

The beginning of Los Angeles was anything but auspicious. Like San Jose in the north, the southern pueblo was ordered into existence by the governor of Alta California, Colonel Felipe de Neve. Both were created as agricultural centers whose roles were to supply food to a seaside military presidio—in L.A.'s case, Santa Barbara. The primary lure of the site was an all-year water source originally named the *Río Porciúncula.* It was a standard, meandering western river, broad in the rainy season but never deep, with undefined banks that slopped over the valleys through which it flowed during the winter months and receded to a much smaller, permanent flow in the summer. It was only subsequent settlers who found that the majority of this river was underground, which led to hundreds of wells being dug and decades of arguments over riparian rights.

The first Europeans to investigate Southern California were in the Gaspar de Portolà expedition in 1769. On August 2, the exploration party made camp at the foot of present-day Elysian Park. Their diarist, Father Juan Crespi, named the fertile land after the previous day, which had been the jubilee day of Our Lady, with a nod toward the founder of his priestly order, the Franciscans. When the boosters got hold of the founding myth, they claimed the place was given the grandiose name *El Pueblo de Nuestra Senora la Reina de Los Angeles de Porciúncula* (The Town of Our Lady Queen of the Angels of Porciúncula—the latter being the "little portion" of the Church in Assisi where St. Francis prayed). The Spaniards who were in charge until the declaration of Mexican independence in 1821 referred to it as *La Reina de Los Angeles* in both their official and popular writings. The *pueblo* simply referred to the type of settlement Los Angeles was, and Porciúncula was a geographic locator for the obscure little town, referencing the name of the local river. The expansive name was often quoted by the boosters, hungry to romanticize L.A.'s mundane early history.

The first settlement in the area was inland toward the mountains and another water

Amateur stereo view of the Los Angeles River, near Elysian Park.

source, the Santa Ana River. San Gabriel was the fourth mission in Alta California, founded on September 8, 1771 and relocated to its present site in 1776. It quickly became one of the most successful in the chain. As agriculturally abundant as the new mission was, the seaside presidios needed still more food. It was only then that Spanish eyes were turned toward Father Crespi's "delightful place among the trees" on the *Río Porciúncula*.

The new Pueblo of Los Angeles, just like hundreds of other small outposts in the Spanish American colonies, was laid out according to Spain's two-hundred-year-old Law of the Indies. Like most such pueblos, Los Angeles was a pretty grim little place. The earliest accounts of the founding of the city were indicative of the boosters' efforts to romanticize the insignificant past of the city to enhance its present. Alice Mary Phillips wrote a history of the city for the 1907 convention of the National Educational Association. She described the September 4, 1781 slog by a bunch of tired settlers as a formal procession that journeyed from Mission San Gabriel flying the banner of the Virgin Mary to found the new pueblo in a "solemn and impressive ceremony" presided over by Governor de Neve himself.

This set the tone for the promotional campaign. Phillips was echoing the 1883 writings of Helen Hunt Jackson, who received the vision from the former mayor and acknowledged leader of the native Californio community, Don Antonio Coronel. He was instrumental in guiding Jackson as she collected stories for what would become her novel, *Ramona*. The founding became even more impressive with each telling by the likes of boosters John Steven

The *campanario* or bell wall is the most famous image of Mission San Gabriel. It was built following the failure of the original bell tower in an 1812 earthquake.

The missions were a constant symbol for the promised romance of Southern California. The author of this small tourist pamphlet invited anyone with questions to come visit him at the Hotel Clark. 1929

Where-to-go
and
What-to-see
in
Southern
California

By P. G. B. MORRISS

McGroarty, Charles Dwight Willard and Harrie Rebecca Forbes, and writers such as Genevieve Solon, Dana Bartlett and Morrow Mayo. The origin of the new pueblo, like its original name, would be given mythic trappings. It was portrayed as a colorful, formal event with bands playing, banners waving, and the noble pioneers marching proudly into their new homes. This fit the boosters' efforts to create an impressive past for L.A., but it was pure fabrication. The truth was that the colonial administrators were hard put to find anyone willing to leave well-settled Mexican states of Sinaloa and Sonora for the wilds of Alta California. The lure of having their own land in the new pueblo finally convinced twelve families to give it a try. Research by historians devoid of the need to inject romance into a mundane situation paints a rather different picture of the founding of Los Angeles. The forty-four original *pobladores*, escorted by the Army wherever they went, walked up from Baja California, retooled and rested at Mission San Gabriel, then walked in at least three groups on different days over to the banks of the *Río Porciúncula* and slowly set up a new town. No banners waving, no mass said, no Governor de Neve present. September 4 was designated as the founding day by the governor for the legal purpose of noting the distribution of land to the new settlers. It was a scene completely lacking in historical romance.

Myth-making was a major component of the promotional campaign; a favorite was the grandeur of the pre-American period the boosters called the "Days of the Dons." This fantasy ignored the Mexican period of control and harked back to a romanticized era when cultured Spaniards—daring horsemen, extravagantly courteous and well-dressed—were the lords of Southern California. They were presented as operating prosperous ranchos, helped by their beautiful wives and daughters and stalwart sons. The Franciscans were their cheerful, dedicated helpers in keeping this mythical land prosperous. The Native Americans were in the background, very quietly doing the menial work, having their souls saved and learning the benefits of European civilization. The myth of course ignored the total destruction of native cultures and the strict social stratification that was endemic to Spanish colonies.

John Steven McGroarty, *Los Angeles Times* editorial writer and eventual congressman and poet laureate of California, was instrumental in spreading the myth through his dramatic work, *The Mission Play*. The melodrama came about through the support of *Los Angeles Times* publisher and leading booster, Harrison Gray Otis. He had been persuaded by Frank Miller, developer of

The back of this postcard of Ramona's Marriage Place has the lyrics of Lee Johnson's song "Ramona." "Ramona, my prairie flower / Ramona, I 'wait the hour / In each star I seem to see / The sweet face of my Indian maid, Ramona." c. 1912

Below: Tourist photo of an old building adjacent to "The Mission Play" Theater and Mission San Gabriel that was falsely identified as Ramona's birthplace. On the back, the traveler referred to it as "Ramona's Home."

Bottom left: My grandfather, Albert Albrecht, with shipmates from the *U.S.S. South Dakota* at what is generically labeled "Ramona's Home." It is the Estudillo adobe in Old Town San Diego which was eventually turned into the tourist extravaganza labeled "Ramona's Marriage Place." 1910

John Steven McGroarty's *The Mission Play* was performed in San Gabriel from 1912 to 1932. He opened his Mission Playhouse in 1927, with his own apartment on the second floor in the front.

Riverside's Mission Inn, to give McGroarty four months paid vacation from the *Times* to write the play. *The Mission Play* was first performed on Mission San Gabriel grounds on April 29, 1912. A new and impressive theater was built near the mission in 1927 to be the permanent home for the production, which centered on the founding, flowering and destruction of the California missions. In McGroarty's influential view, "The days of the Missions mark the golden age of California. In that wonderful time everybody was happy, well fed and content. Nobody was poor. Nobody was rich. It was an age of easy toil, of prayer and song and laughter, of peace and an existence wholly ideal."

Father Junipero Serra, founder and Superior of the missions of Alta California, was a much-revered character in the Days of the Dons stories. Father Zephyrin Engelhardt, a

The formal portrait of the members of Tilton's Trolley Trip.

Left: From a set of tourist cards illustrating the various sights around Los Angeles. It notes the mission "is seven miles from Los Angeles and is on the Pacific Electric car line." c. 1912

The stairs to the choir loft and the bell wall of Mission San Gabriel. This photograph was sold in the Mission Curio Store.

Postcard view of the Plaza and the "Old Mission Church." The back text notes that the Plaza was "for a great many years the civic center of the city." Regardless of the look and text, the Plaza Church was never a mission—except to the boosters. c. 1915

Program for the play *Jimmy, Jr.* at Oliver Morosco's Burbank Theater on Main Street. The play had a contemporary theme that had nothing at all to do with the Days of the Dons. July 1911

Right: Part of the 150th anniversary of the founding of Los Angeles at Mission San Gabriel. 1931

Franciscan historian writing during the height of the promotional campaign, was effusive in his praise of both the founder and all the Franciscans working for him. He noted the priests of the missions "did not appear on this western coast in order to enrich themselves; for all, in accordance with their vow of poverty, died at their post or returned to the mother-house in Mexico as poor as they had come." The priests had the added burden of trying to convert "a race of people who did not reason, whose thoughts turned on nothing higher than how to fill their stomach."

This summed up the prevalent opinion about the indigenous Shoshonean-speaking Native Americans, whom the Spaniards labeled *Gabrieleños* (after the mission). They were almost universally reviled as being entry-level human beings, at best. Writing in 1892, Kate Sanborn called them "repulsive stolid creatures . . . with sullen stare, long be-vermined locks, and filthy blankets full of fleas." She hoped they could be improved someday, but for her they were "a species of monkey; he imitates and copies white men, but selects vice in preference to virtue." McGroarty, as a dedicated booster, knew the reason for the Native Americans' lack of perceived civilization. "They

Don Jose Antonio Arillo, chief character in Percival Cooney's 1914 novel, *Dons of the Old Pueblo.*

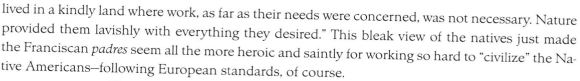

lived in a kindly land where work, as far as their needs were concerned, was not necessary. Nature provided them lavishly with everything they desired." This bleak view of the natives just made the Franciscan *padres* seem all the more heroic and saintly for working so hard to "civilize" the Native Americans—following European standards, of course.

The single most famous book written about early Southern California was one of the few to take a darker view of the Native American's fate at the hands of the Yankee conquerors. Helen Hunt Jackson wrote her famed *Ramona* after completing *A Century of Dishonor* (1881), her book on the wrongs visited upon Native Americans. *The Century* magazine commissioned her to write a series of four articles about Southern California. During the research trip she also developed the ideas and scouted the locales for a book that she hoped would do for Native Americans what Harriet Beecher Stowe's *Uncle Tom's Cabin* had done for African Americans. The resulting historical romance, *Ramona,* was published in 1884.

The story line of *Ramona* is a sad one. Americans have taken over Southern California and an entire way of life is disappearing. The spring verdure of Southern California is still "like nothing in nature except the glitter of a brilliant lizard in the sun or the iridescent sheen of a peacock's neck." But everything else has changed. A lone Franciscan priest travels from ruined mission to collapsing rancho. The relaxed days of Spanish control are gone. Ramona's Native American husband, Alessandro, is thoughtlessly killed by an Anglo who thought Alessandro had stolen his horse. The killing breaks the heart of the beautiful and faithful Ramona. Justice is never served since Alessandro was "only an injun." Ramona eventually marries her stepbrother, Felipe, and they leave American-dominated California for Mexico.

Ramona and its supposed locales became key points on the Southern California tourist itinerary relentlessly pushed by the boosters. But Helen Hunt Jackson was not alone as an activist for celebrating the Southland's Spanish past. Charles Fletcher Lummis, who became city editor of the *Times* and later editor of the magazine *Land of Sunshine*, was instrumental in starting the Landmarks Club in 1895, an organization dedicated to saving the largely abandoned and crumbling California missions. In the mid-1920s Christine Sterling convinced Harry Chandler and the Chamber of Commerce to help her save Olvera Street and the Plaza as a memorial to the beginnings of the city. Her efforts saved the most historic part of Los Angeles from being leveled to accommodate "progress." *El Paseo de Los Angeles* opened on Easter Sunday, April 19, 1930.

Despite all the eventual romanticizing of the city's past by its boosters, when Los Angeles became an American city in 1850 it was the kind of wide-open, lawless town that would be portrayed in hundreds of Hollywood movies sixty years later. English traveler Sir George Simpson labeled L.A. "the abode of the lowest drunkards and gamblers in the country." The town was full of Gold Rush rejects and the local hills were home to a succession of Mexican bandits. Murder and mayhem were so common that L.A. was often popularly referred to as Lost Angels or Los Diablos. In the twenty-year period after statehood in 1850, the Los Angeles population grew only from 1,610 to 5,798. As Charles Nordhoff noted in his 1873 account of life in California, "The town of

Christine Sterling always meant for Olvera Street to be a celebration of Los Angeles as it existed during the Days of the Dons. She described her vision of the Spanish period: "Life in Los Angeles before the Americans came was an almost ideal existence. People lived to love, to be kind, tolerant and contented. Money, of which there was plenty, was just for necessities. The men owned and rode magnificent horses. The women were flower-like in silk and laces. There were picnics into the hills, dancing at night, moonlight serenades, romance and real happiness."

Lucretia del Valle was a member of the family that owned Rancho Camulos in Ventura County. Helen Hunt Jackson spent two hours there while doing research for what would become *Ramona*. Her descriptions of the home Ramona lived in came from here. The del Valle family packed produce under the Home of Ramona brand. Lucretia del Valle appeared in more than eight hundred fifty performances of John Steven McGroarty's *The Mission Play*, wearing her grandmother's gowns.

Bottom right: Harrie Rebecca Piper Smith Forbes (Mrs. A.S.C. Forbes) was a key figure in celebrating the Southland's Spanish heritage. She was the head of the Los Angeles Camera Club and its Salons and wrote *Mission Tales in the Days of the Dons* (1909) as well as other books and numerous articles. She was also an officer in the Landmarks Club and came up with the idea of placing mission bells along *El Camino Real*, convinced the Chamber of Commerce to support the idea, and then designed and manufactured more than 425 that were put in place between 1906 and 1913.

From the fiesta scene from the second act of *The Mission Play* at Mission San Carlos de Carmelo. Act Two presented the California missions at their apogee.

Left: Dancing "*El Sombrero Blanco*" at Carmelo during the fiesta scene. According to legend, Father Serra himself composed the dance of the white hat. According to the play's program, the dance and music will make you "rhythm-mad."

the angels is not a very angelic place."

Clearly, this was not an era boosters extolled while trying to encourage immigration, so it was largely ignored in the promotional literature. Los Angeles in the 1870s was just another frontier city with unpaved streets, few large buildings, and little to recommend it other than its agricultural markets. After the Southern Pacific arrived in 1876, its promotional literature minimized the chaos of the primitive city and concentrated on its climate and the healthful life it afforded, agricultural prosperity, cheap cost of living and its scenic beauty. Among the most widely distributed publications from this era were special issues of newspapers, Board of Trade pamphlets, Charles Nordhoff's extremely influential *California: A Book for Travelers and Settlers* and Charles Dudley Warner's *Our Italy*, which is a hymn to the climate and physical diversity of Southern California.

One unique book available in both the United States and Europe during this earliest promotional era was the result of the insatiable curiosity of Prince Ludwig Louis Salvator, archduke of Austria and a world traveler of the first order. He was curious about the place

Self-portrait of Charles Fletcher Lummis at the home he built near the Arroyo Seco, El Alisal (The Sycamore). Harris Newmark referred to him as "long a distinguished and always a picturesquely recognizable resident." 1911

Dolores del Rio, front and center, who was to star in the movie *Ramona*, posing with the cast of the Hemet play. 1928

At the corner of Calle de los Negros on the Plaza. This building is typical of the structures Lieutenant Edward O.C. Ord saw when he came to Los Angeles in 1849 to draw the first map of the city. He recalled his initial impression: "After winding through the willow hedgerows for a couple of miles, we drove suddenly out from among the vineyards and gardens and in among rows of flat one-storied adobe houses with long corridors in front covering the side walk. Melted bitumen was dripping from the flat roofs to the danger of careless pedestrians. Turning a corner, the rows of houses took the shape of streets of shops. One street led to the Plaza, whence two or three others branched, and this was the City of Los Angeles."

The Romance of Centinela Springs was first produced in 1931 at the Inglewood Bowl in Centinela Park. It told the story of Spaniards discovering the Springs and their threat to wrestle them from the local Indians. Warfare is averted when the Spanish cavalier falls in love with the chief's daughter, Princess Centinela, and is swayed to a peaceful path by the wisdom of her father. 1932

Below: The Ramona pageant started at Hemet in 1923 and continues.

that had been described to him as the healthiest part of the United States. The book that resulted from his 1875 visit, one of at least thirty-five he published, was called *A Flower of the Golden Land of Los Angeles*. Sounding like a Chamber of Commerce pamphlet from forty years in the future, Prince Ludwig noted, the climate "of Los Angeles . . . is especially balmy. Indeed, the climate in Southern California . . . is such that it is surpassed by no other region in the new world. Extremes of heat and cold are unknown; it is a land of perpetual spring. In winter, the days are invariably comfortably warm; the nights, in summer, are delightfully cool—blankets, as a matter of fact, being essential at night throughout the summer season."

These early publications were only a mild harbinger of what was to come. So numerous

Bernice Claire, an actress and singer with First National Pictures, posing at Mission San Fernando in the romantic, booster view of the Spanish past. This was in sharp contrast to the hard-bitten frontier town Lt. Edward Ord visited. 1929

Dolores del Rio and Rita Carewe cool off during the location filming of *Ramona*. Some of the exteriors were photographed in the Hemet area, while the film crew had to go all the way to Utah to find a sufficiently large herd of sheep. This, of course, was not advertised by the production company. Moviegoers of the 1920s assumed everything was filmed in the Los Angeles area. 1928

were the articles about Los Angeles during the boom of the 1880s, that an 1885 article in the *San Jose Times-Mercury* complained, "Our brethren of the city and would-be state of the Angels understand how to advertise. The average Eastern mind conceives of California as a small tract of country situated in and about Los Angeles." But they hadn't seen anything yet.

The inaccessibility that had plagued Los Angeles since its inception changed in 1876 because of a successful campaign using land and money—plenty of both—to entice the Southern Pacific to build a very difficult line south to Los Angeles, connecting obscure towns to the transcontinental railroad system. The rest of the United States would soon be hearing all about the paradise to be found in sunny Southern California for the price of a train ticket and a dream.

Harrie Forbes convinced the city to formally name the viaducts over the Los Angeles River after figures in California history. The Ninth Street Viaduct (which like Tenth Street was altered and renamed for the 1932 Olympics) is officially the Gaspar de Portolà Viaduct. The Chamber of Commerce created a fiesta for the September 26, 1925 christening that celebrated the Days of the Dons. The *Times* noted the festival brought back "memories of ancient Spanish fiestas, of the days when Los Angeles laughed with the full freedom of her careless youth."

Right: Chamber officers are in costume to dance the *Jota* at the festival.

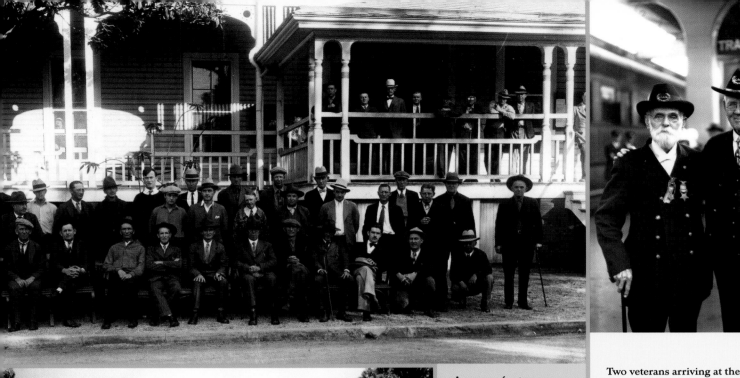

A group of veterans gathered outside Barracks I at the Soldiers' Home at Sawtelle.

Right: Garden City photo of a float celebrating Abraham Lincoln on its way downtown from the Solidiers' Home for a La Fiesta parade. c. 1896

Below: Barracks building for Company L and the surrounding cactus garden. 1911

Two veterans arriving at the Southern Pacific station for the encampment of the Grand Army of the Republic. 1926

Entrance gate to the Veterans' Cemetery. The crossbeam above the road has part of Theodore O'Hara's 1847 poem, "The Bivouac of the Dead." It was written to commemorate Kentuckians killed at the Battle of Buena Vista in the Mexican War, but was very commonly used in Civil War cemeteries. The quote is from the first stanza. "On fame's eternal camping ground / Their silent tents are spread. / And glory guards with silent round / The bivouac of the dead."

Right: A 1907 pamphlet about the National Home for Disabled Volunteer Soldiers. The various National Soldiers' Homes were available only for Union soldiers and veterans of the Indian Wars. Former Confederate soldiers were cared for by private societies.

CHAPTER TWO

The Private Car Tracks below the Central Station were a small part of the huge Los Angeles Coach Yard located east of the station. The yard had its own Baldwin switch engine to separate the Pullman, coaches and dining cars of the twenty to thirty daily passenger trains. The number of coach cars for the named trains— such as the overnight *Lark* to San Francisco or the *Golden State Limited* to Chicago—remained fairly constant, but often Pullman cars had to be added at the last minute due to ticket sales. So as many as fifty Pullman cars would be stored in the Coach Yard at any given time.

SOUTHERN PACIFIC'S CENTRAL STATION

Southern Pacific's barnlike Arcade Depot was replaced by the elegant, Italian Renaissance-style Central Station on June 12, 1915. Indicative of the growth in Los Angeles, the new station could handle sixteen passenger trains at a time, while its predecessor had space for three. This was important because within three years of its opening, Central Station saw 1,400,000 passengers passing through its doors. Union Pacific joined Southern Pacific at the Central Station in 1923. Both left for Union Station in 1939.

Santa Fe's Moorish-inspired La Grande Station opened in 1893 on Santa Fe Avenue between Second and Third Streets. One of its last uses as a train station was as a gathering point where Japanese Americans were shuttled on Pacific Electric cars to the Assembly Center built in the parking lot of Santa Anita Racetrack, where they were forced to stay prior to being sent to internment camps. La Grande was torn down in 1946 to make way for a freight terminal.

SANTA FE'S LA GRANDE STATION

Santa Fe's La Grande Station was that line's Los Angeles point of debarkation throughout the promotional campaign. The Moorish-looking building opened on July 29, 1893. Its signature dome had to be removed due to damage from the 1933 earthquake. Santa Fe's passenger service was transferred to the new Union Station upon its opening on May 7, 1939. Santa Fe's emblematic Harvey House restaurant followed the line's trains to Union Station.

Here is our Mediterranean! Here is our Italy! It is a Mediterranean without marshes and without malaria . . . It is a Mediterranean with a more equable climate, warmer winters and cooler summers . . . The time is not distant when this corner of the United States will produce in abundance, and year after year without failure, all the fruits and nuts which for a thousand years the civilized world of Europe has looked to the Mediterranean to supply."

Charles Dudley Warner, *Our Italy,* 1891

Los Angeles was a minor agricultural town when California became a state in 1850. Thanks to the Gold Rush, San Francisco and Sacramento had rapidly developed into established American frontier cities, but the southern part of the state was a series of ranchos still held over from the Spanish land-grant days. The city in the middle of all those ranches was little more than a rude collection of adobe buildings with a smattering of wooden structures. None of its streets were paved. The town was lighted haphazardly by oil lamps that the citizenry was required by law to light at night. Life was very cheap, with murders in 1853 occurring in the town of roughly four thousand people at the rate of one a week. Water was supplied by the *Zanja Madre* (Mother Ditch), an irrigation canal that flowed from the Los Angeles River and various artesian wells located near the town. The *zanjaros* were the men who controlled the flow of the canals, and charged homeowners and farmers according to their usage. Even Harry Carr, whose 1935 book *Los Angeles: City of Dreams* was generally a poem of praise, called the 1850s city "a vile little dump."

Two major events brought about the change in the small town and set the stage for the promotional campaign to come. What leading merchant and dedicated diarist Harris Newmark called "an annihilating drought," in the years 1857 and 1858—and one that was even worse from 1862 to 1864—brought an end to the era of the ranchos. Newmark noted sadly, "The suffering of the poor animals beggars description." Cattle died by the thousands in the Southland and ranch owners lost their land to speculators, the banks and other lenders. The second event was the most significant one in the history of Los Angeles—the arrival of a transcontinental railroad branch line from San Francisco. Los Angeles was so insignificant that the Southern Pacific's original plan was to bypass it by putting the main line through San Bernardino and continuing on to San Diego. The effect of the coming of the railroad to any town in the West was abundantly clear by 1876. Harris Newmark noted of the small town that it was of the "most vital importance to her future

Welcoming a friend or relative at the La Grande Station—a scene enacted tens of thousands of times during the promotional era. c. 1919

prosperity and growth" to convince Collis P. Huntington (who, along with Charles Crocker, Leland Stanford and Mark Hopkins composed railroad's "Big Four," the co-founders of the Southern Pacific Railway) to run the S.P. to Los Angeles.

Real-estate entrepreneur Robert Widney realized the supremacy of the railroad as the catalyst for future development of western towns. He used every political and promotional tactic possible to persuade his fellow Angelenos that their future depended on making it worthwhile for the S.P. to lay track to Los Angeles. But the cost was not minimal. The S.P. required a payment of five percent of the county's assessed valuation, which amounted to $610,000. Land, as always with the railroad, was part of the deal—so much land that the S.P. eventually became one of the largest property owners in Los Angeles County. This included not only the right of way into the city but also several acres in the heart of the central city for a depot. The last part of the agreement took in another aspect of early railroads: eliminating competition. The city was required to surrender the twenty-two miles of track of Phineas Banning's Los Angeles and San Pedro Railroad.

To seal the deal, the original, short-lived Chamber of Commerce took it upon itself to send

Jack Riley was the conductor on the first Southern Pacific train to arrive in Los Angeles. Photo taken by one of the leading photographers in the city, Valentin Wolfenstein. September 5, 1876.

Above right: Santa Fe engines lined up at the La Grande Station. c. 1926

a telegram, which Newmark noted cost seventy-five dollars due to its "eloquence and length," to the United States Senate with the hope of inducing that body to help Los Angeles' cause. Given the enormous amount of land granted to the railroads by Congress, pressure from the Senate was no small measure. With all its demands met, and a chance to make Congressional leaders happy, the railroad agreed to include Los Angeles on the transcontinental line. The largest obstacle along the route was the San Fernando Pass south of Newhall. Blasting and digging work went on for a year and a half, and resulted in the longest tunnel west of the Mississippi River. A golden spike was driven by Charles Crocker on September 6, 1876, near John Lang's Hotel at Lang's Station northeast of Newhall in Soledad Canyon. Suddenly, Los Angeles was connected to the rest of the country.

The arrival of the Southern Pacific made Los Angeles far more accessible to prospective settlers. Connection to the transcontinental line helped fuel the first Los Angeles land boom—further stoking a real-estate bonanza that had been underway since Mexican land-grant ranchos were broken up into family farms. The first L.A. Chamber of Commerce issued several broadsides to be distributed in the East and Midwest. They were typically unillustrated, text-driven, nineteenth-century advertising sheets which used many statistics to extol the unprecedented opportunity awaiting farmers who relocated to L.A.

Among his many other accomplishments, Robert Widney was the first real-estate entrepreneur in Los Angeles. The 1870s land boom provided him with a great deal of competition. New towns and developments started springing up all over the Los Angeles plain. But the worst drought in a decade helped bust that boom. The vast grain fields of Los Angeles County shriveled and the sheep industry that had replaced the cattle business was decimated as a general depression settled over the entire state. Land barons, speculators, and ordinary people were ruined. The Los Angeles economy was so shattered that the first Chamber of Commerce closed its doors in 1877.

The second and much greater land rush to Los Angeles occurred after the arrival of the Santa Fe Railroad in 1885. This second transcontinental line entered the city through the Cajon Pass above San Bernardino and set off a rate war with the Southern Pacific. Both railroads were in business to make money, but both also realized that even greater profits could be theirs if they engaged in the loss leader of cutting rates. The cost of travel to the coast from Kansas City fell for months, famously reaching one dollar for a few hours on March 6, 1887. Given the amount of free publicity and the number of passengers this garnered, it was a worthy endeavor for the railroads.

Even more land changed hands than in the previous decade, as dozens of towns and neighborhoods were platted, but the city did not suffer the same financial debacle that happened after the first of the land rushes. Local banks, led by Isaias Hellman's Farmers and Merchants Bank, were steadfastly conservative in their lending policies. They steadily increased the number of loans while decreasing the percentage of deposits risked on those loans. The drought and bank failures that marked the collapse of the boom of the 1870s did not materialize this time.

There were many lasting effects of the 1880s boom. Chief among them was the final breakup of the ranchos and an increase in population from eleven thousand to fifty thousand Angelenos. Los Angeles began to look truly like an "American" city, with paved roads, streetcars, and Romanesque buildings. A new Chamber of Commerce was organized in 1888 and soon became the pre-eminent business and promotional organization in the city.

Despite the growth of Los Angeles and the rate wars, the majority of the booster material issued by the Southern Pacific Railroad was oriented toward the more settled northern part of the state that it had been advertising for a decade. The Los Angeles Chamber of Commerce joined the railroad-supported Immigration Aid Association, California Immigration Union and the California State Board of Trade, all of which, despite their inclusive names, concentrated on the north. This was the case with Southern Pacific publications such as *California Guide for Tourists and Settlers* (1889), *California: Its Attractions for the Invalid, Tourist, Capitalist and Homeseeker* (1890) and *California for Health, Pleasure and Profit: Why You Should Go There* (1893). When the southern part of the state was mentioned, the stress was always on its wonderful climate and bountiful agriculture.

A later indicator of the perfidy of the north running up against the dynamism of the south was the famous "California on Wheels" train exhibit. The original edition of the mobile

Robert Widney arrived in L.A. in 1867 and opened a combination law and real-estate office. He went from being the city's first real-estate agent to starting its first streetcar line, then became a judge and helped to found the first Chamber of Commerce and the University of Southern California. Widney led the fight to convince the populace to pay the dunning demanded by the Southern Pacific to come to Los Angeles, saved a Chinese man from a lynching during the riots of 1871 and did much of the preliminary design work on the harbor at San Pedro.

Left: Santa Fe ad from *Life*, 1904

County Courthouse under construction. The small building in the foreground is the former St. Athanasius, built in 1864 as the first Protestant house of worship in L.A. In 1883 it was sold to the county and used for offices as part of Court House Square until it was torn down after the opening of the new County Building.

In the late nineteenth century, Western county seats with ambition built an imposing Richardsonian Romanesque courthouse. Los Angeles was no exception. L.A. County Building opened on Poundcake Hill at Broadway and Temple Streets in 1891. It was the predominant civic building illustrated by the boosters until the new City Hall opened in 1928.

The first County Building, on the left, was originally built by John Temple as a market and theater in 1859, but the county bought it soon after it was completed. Here the Rev. Elias Birdsall delivered an oration and prayers for the murdered Abraham Lincoln, The new courthouse on the hill fit the city that emerged from the boom of the 1880s. c. 1890

The Civic Center, including the Hall of Justice and County Building, seen through Spring Street columns of the new City Hall. 1929

Ad reproduced in a Union Pacific pamphlet that printed the dialog from the U.P.-sponsored radio program, "Romance of Transportation."

Center: Union Pacific ad from *McClure's Magazine.* January, 1910

Give the Union Pacific publicity department credit for this 1929 pamphlet. It takes a significant amount of chutzpah to sell the "mystery and romance" of a place called Death.

Below: The Union Pacific's *Los Angeles Limited* promised to be "unsurpassed in speed, appointments and service between Chicago and Southern California." 1926

promotion was developed by the California State Board of Trade. This businessman's organization, inaugurated in 1887 to unify the state promotional efforts, was largely started by San Francisco businessmen, and reflected that fact. The Board's first big booster effort was a free exhibit that would travel from town to town in the Midwest and Northeast in three railroad coaches with vestibules displaying California agricultural products and distributing literature.

The exhibit's premiere run in 1888 was one of the first times Southern California, represented by the Los Angeles Chamber of Commerce, cooperated with the state organization. The progress of the train was carefully noted in the *Times,* as was the constant fretting by the Chamber over getting the best agricultural products available. But the bulk of the products and literature on the initial run reflected the northern bias of the State Board of Trade. For the subsequent 1891 tour, Frank Wiggins, the Chamber's new director of publicity, so completely redesigned and stocked the cars with the bountiful products of Southland agriculture that he is generally credited with inventing the whole "California on Wheels" concept. Much to the north's chagrin, it was Wiggins and the Chamber who had the formula for making the traveling exhibit exciting and, more importantly, successful.

The railroads did, of course, advertise Southern California. The Southern Pacific paid for Charles Nordhoff's *California: A Book for Travelers and Settlers* (1873) which had seven chapters devoted to the southern part of the state and was the single most influential booster publication of the nineteenth century. Once the line was guaranteed to be extended to Los Angeles, the

Right: It wasn't just the Chamber of Commerce and the Realty Board that pushed colonization in Southern California. In 1926, the Santa Fe promised settlers that they would find "The Land of Opportunity for those who seek new homes in a delightful climate, where a good living can be made on small ranches and fruit farms. Fertile soil, enough water, and practically no winter."

Tehachapi was always significant to the Southern Pacific, not only because it was the demarcation line for the milder weather of Southern California, but also because the mountain range had to be conquered to finish the line south. This guide to the towns and attractions of the Southland was published in 1904. The three previous editions had already been distributed to 180,000 interested customers.

As usual, jobbing shops and restaurants grew up around the train station. This is the huge, barn-like Arcade Station of the Southern Pacific. The glorious palm tree in front of it is now in Exposition Park in front of the Coliseum. The photo is by J.B. Blanchard, whose studio produced the finest of the "views" available to tourists. He also invented the description "Los Angeles and Vicinity in Mid-Winter," which fit the booster ethic perfectly while helping to sell photos.

railroad hired local newsman Benjamin Truman to write *Semi-Tropical California* (1876). He went on to write several pamphlets as director of the Southern Pacific's Literary Bureau: *A Southern California Paradise* (1883), *In Semi-Tropical California* (1893), and *California: South of Tehachapi* (1903). The Santa Fe, with less of a stake in Northern California, tended to stress the south in booklets such as Charles Keeler's *Southern California* (1899), *California Picture Book* (reprinted throughout the 1920s and 1930s). *California: The Golden State*, from the Rock Island Line in 1910, emphasized the south as well.

Southern Pacific also made a point of funding many of the earliest booster groups. This was particularly true of the Immigration Association of California and the State Board of Trade. Their largess extended south of the Tehachapis to the Southern California Immigration Association and the early work of both of the Los Angeles Chambers of Commerce. The railroad's literary arm also published *Sunset* magazine, which, after 1900, featured hundreds of articles and advertisements to boost California's many attractions.

A significant number of the new settlers in the 1870s and 1880s were health seekers coming to take the "California Cure." Many of them were "lungers" suffering from tuberculosis, which was commonly known as consumption in the nineteenth century. At that time little was known about how to

Hotel Arcadia in Santa Monica was the first of the area's grand seaside hotels. Opened on January 25, 1887 and lasting until 1909, it is infamous in the annals of L.A. crime as the site where Colonel Griffith J. Griffith—who donated the land for one of the largest urban parks in America—shot his wife in 1904. The photo was taken by local photographer H.F. Rile, whose studio is seen on the beach at left.

cure the disease. One of the few treatments was to send the consumptive to a dry, warm climate—most frequently New Mexico or Southern California—to either recover or die.

"Trying California" became the last, best hope for thousands of out-of-options patients who flocked to the Southland. Sanatorium after sanatorium was built throughout the Southland in the 1870s and 1880s. Ojai, San Diego, and Monrovia were home to several, and San Bernardino and Redlands were part of what came to be called the "Great Orange and Sanatorium Belt." In 1873 Charles Nordhoff included an appendix on "Southern California for Consumptives" in his California guide book. It consisted of a very long letter from his friend Francis Miles, who had sought relief for his tuberculosis at several places in southern Europe and Florida ("too damp") before he tried California. Miles wrote, "Southern California presents a most glowingly invigorating tonic and stimulating climate, very much superior to anything I know of, the air is so pure and so much drier than . . . elsewhere." He goes on to prove his claims with six pages of tables demonstrating the region's healthful superiority.

In 1894, Newton Chittenden echoed Miles's sentiment in his *Health Seekers, Tourists and Sportsmen's Guide to Health and Pleasure Resorts of the Pacific Coast*. Noting that he had consulted both experts and sufferers, he concluded that:

California Hospital, 1414 S. Hope Street. This was both a general hospital and a sanatorium. 1902

The Arcade Depot was one of the last of the Southern Pacific's large wooden stations. The Queen Anne-style building was designed by the S.P.'s buildings-and-bridges superintendent, Arthur Brown, and opened on Alameda Street in 1888 on the site of a former orange grove.

The depots of the Los Angeles and Salt Lake Railroad and the Santa Fe were opposite one another, separated by the Los Angeles River.

Below: Interior of the 1915 Southern Pacific station. The Union Pacific Railroad joined the S.P. at Central Station in 1923 after it bought out the Los Angeles and Salt Lake Railroad. The old Salt Lake station was in poor shape to begin with, and a 1923 fire put the nail in its coffin.

Main entrance to Central Station at Fifth and Central, which was the L.A. base for the Southern Pacific and Union Pacific. It was the most expensive station west of Kansas City. c. 1926

Southern California probably affords the most perfect conditions of climate, combined with other advantages, for a home for consumptives of any portion of North America. These are a dry, pure equable, stimulating atmosphere, the most sunshine, the greatest choice of situations, as to elevation, humidity and exposure in conjunction with superior advantages for engaging in light, pleasant and profitable occupations.

One of the several medical doctors writing on the subject was Dr. William Edwards. In his book, *Two Health-Seekers in Southern California* (1897), he stressed the benefits of the local sanatoriums:

Speaking broadly, persons suffering from any of the following conditions will find certain locations in Southern California to be useful aids in restoring them to health—incipient or early phthisis or tuberculosis in any form, chronic pneumonia or a tardy convalescence from either pneumonia or pleurisy, diseases of the liver following malarial poison, cirrhosis of the liver, simple congestion or hepatic catarrh, jaundice, functional disturbances, and organic ills in those of advanced years and weak or poorly-nourished children.

In general, Edwards promised readers that they would find in the Southland "a most soothing climate to regain their lost energy or restore the nervous system to its normal equilibrium."

Many of the key players in the promotional campaign first came to Los Angeles as health

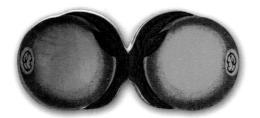

seekers. Frank Wiggins is at the top of that list. The longtime secretary of the Chamber of Commerce was near death when he took the train from Indiana to replace another lunger, Charles Dwight Willard, as the Chamber secretary. Willard had initially written for the *Times* and the *Herald*. He later started the magazine *Land of Sunshine*. Charles Lummis, another survivor who was cured by the air of Los Angeles, would help found the Southwest Museum and the Landmarks Club. Harry Chandler, who recovered his health in Los Angeles, also went to work for the *Times* and eventually married publisher Harrison Gray Otis's daughter Marian. Chandler went on to become one of the major land developers in Los Angeles and chief founder of the All Year Club that induced Southland tourism.

Most of the people who took the climate cure in Southern California and survived were known only to their friends and relatives, but became part of the positive statistics the Chamber was so fond of quoting. On the flip side of this coin were the grim mortality rates. Once the railroads started promoting Southern California, they warned people to ignore the life expectancy rates published about Los Angeles: too many people who came west were at death's door, only to pass through it while in L.A.

After the turn of the twentieth century, support for indigent health seekers rapidly waned in Southern California. By 1900 the influx of completely healthy people arriving every day had negated the need to attract sick ones. Promoters stopped publicizing the area as a recuperative spot and the sanatoriums either were closed, turned into hotels or torn down to build more traditional housing.

Also waning by the second decade of the new century was the role of the railroads' publications in the Southern California boosterism scene. However, the railroads still played an important role by transporting the goods for pro-L.A. exhibitions that were set up throughout the country. By the early twentieth century, the Chamber was the leading promotional organization in the country and no longer needed anyone to show it how to publicize its city, and by extension, all of Southern California.

Souvenir of the Salt Lake Route, 1915. The Los Angeles and Salt Lake Railroad was a third main line arriving in L.A. in 1905. Union Pacific Railroad always had part ownership in the line and absorbed it in 1923.

Below: Riverside Chamber of Commerce greeters welcome *Los Angeles Limited* passengers to the fruitful Southland. January, 1926

CHAPTER THREE

While you are throwing snow balls,
Oranges I'm eating;
'Neath skies of blue I'm far from you,
From winter cold retreating.

An Orange Orchard in beautiful California.

On the back of this postcard a woman wrote, "Yesterday at Pasadena looked through an orange grove at the snow-capped mountains. This reminded me of it." The images may have been enhanced, but they weren't just booster fantasies. c. 1910

ORANGES AND SNOW

Blooming orange groves with snow-capped mountains in the distance was the perfect shorthand for the boosters' view of Southern California. Climate on the plain would remain mild, while those who craved "normal" winter could go visit it in the mountains where it belonged. Oranges represented not only the mild, semi-tropical climate of the region but also the health and vigor of the "Climatic Capital of the Nation." The oranges-and-mountains motif also set Southern California apart from Florida. The highest point in that bug-ridden state is 345 feet.

Actress Mary Miles Minter, second from right, came down to the Chamber of Commerce, with her mother at her side, to say goodbye to outgoing president S.L. Weaver. Frank Wiggins, right, the face of the Chamber, was there for the press photographer. June 4, 1921

FRANK WIGGINS

Frank Wiggins. The very face and spirit of the promotional campaign. In his novel about the Harbor fight, *Rose of Los Angeles,* John Campbell described the Chamber secretary. "He had a magnetic smile and warm clasp to his hand. When he talked of Los Angeles, his eyes glowed with earnestness . . . [he was] a preacher of the gospel of Los Angeles." He not only dreamed up endless ways to advertise the city, he found ways to carry them out. On Wiggins' death, Chamber president William Lacy noted in a broadside to the membership, "If you would seek his monument, just look around you."

Many Americans who have become weary of the constant struggle for existence in mercantile pursuits, a struggle which is growing more onerous from year to year, cherish a longing for a small farm, in some pleasant section of the country, where, under sunny skies, they may support their families in comfort, and end their days in peace, without being disturbed by the shadow of the sheriff or the poorhouse. There is no section of the United States in which this ideal may be so well realized as in Los Angeles County.

Chamber of Commerce, *Los Angeles City and County,* 1900

W ith a population topping fifty thousand, a Romanesque City Hall and County Building and paved downtown streets, Los Angeles emerged from the Boom of the 1880s as a bona fide American city. It also had a new organization that would coalesce all the efforts to expand the economic and population base of the Southland—the second Los Angeles Chamber of Commerce. Peter Clark MacFarland captured the role the new organization came to play in a 1915 *Collier's Magazine* article:

> The empire builders organized something, and called it a Chamber of Commerce. Chambers of Commerce are common. This one is uncommon. Possibly it is the most efficient of its kind in the world. . . . It built the city. It even picked out the kind of people it wanted to live in the city—the well-to-do farmers, merchants and mechanics of the Mississippi Valley—men close enough to the pioneer line to have courage, initiative and adaptability. Having picked them out, it went after them with sureness of aim . . . and it got them.

The initial meeting of the new Chamber of Commerce was held on October 15, 1888 in the assembly room of the Board of Trade, above the de Turk Livery Stable at First and Fort (later Broadway) streets. From the beginning it was plain that the new Chamber envisioned itself as not just representing the growth and protection of the business interests, but in attracting new settlers. Colonel Harrison Gray Otis, publisher of the *Los Angeles Times* and one of the leaders in organizing the meeting, argued that the "business men and citizens of the City and County of Los

A Few Nuts
And
How to Crack Them

By Frank Wiggins

Published By
The Los Angeles Chamber of Commerce
1915

Frank Wiggins was more an organizer than a writer. He wrote *A Few Nuts* as a straightforward guide to growing walnuts, peanuts and almonds in Southern California.

Angeles are in favor of inducing immigration, stimulating legitimate home industries and establishing favorable home manufacturers." His view resonated with the new organization. When the
Chamber first published its bylaws, the fifth was to "induce immigration to bring about the subdivision, settlement and cultivation of our lands."

Five months later the Chamber moved to its second, more substantial headquarters on
First Street, fittingly right next to Colonel Otis' *Los Angeles Times* building. The first publication the
Chamber distributed around the country was ten thousand copies of its neighbor's *Mid-Winter* edition. All the Los Angeles newspapers published these special editions that were pure boosterism,
with special sections on the development of Southern California, but the *Times* had the biggest
and best. These not only extolled the local agriculture industry, they also wrote about how to get
to the sunny Southland.

The Chamber's first self-generated publication was issued in December 1888 and was
called straightforwardly, *Los Angeles County—Facts and Figures from the Chamber of Commerce*.
Under "Los Angeles City," the pamphlet truculently complains about the "systematic and persistent misrepresentation of this city." Several stories had appeared in eastern publications, all of
which concentrated on "the Busted Boom." True, there had been intense land speculation two
years prior, and the growth had been less than prudent. But, as the Chamber noted,

> The adjustment of values necessarily following speculation has gone quietly but steadily
> forward. No city in the United States ever passed through such a boom and came out of

Everything about Los Angeles needed to be created to make it a major city. Agriculture thrived only due to an extensive system of irrigation. The harbor from which much of the farm product was shipped had to be created from a series of mudflats. No part of the harbor has been subject to more tinkering than Terminal Island. In the photo above, the Badger Avenue Bascule Bridge connecting Terminal Island with the mainland has just been completed while a dredge works in the Cerritos Channel. In 1930 a Ford plant will be opened east of the bridge. In 1941 a Navy base will be constructed on the island and a decade later the *U.S.S. Tuscarora* will be anchored west of the bridge. The great ship had seventy-seven decks and a glass bottom that you could look through and see the fishes swimming by. My grandfather, Chief Petty Office Albert Albrecht, loved that ship. He often pointed it out to me and I always saw it. Seventy-seven decks. How could you miss it? 1924

Small fold-out publication of the Chamber. These would be available at the Chamber headquarters, the branch offices in Chicago and Atlantic City, and at the Los Angeles exhibit at whatever event the Chamber visited.

it as Los Angeles has. . . . We now have a population of seventy-five thousand intelligent, energetic, wide-awake people, who have confidence in the future of Los Angeles.

The back of the broadside is a chart that describes the dozens of crops that can be grown in the Los Angeles area, in which parts of the County they can be grown, what the various soils are like, whether irrigation is necessary and the distance to the closest branch line of a railroad. Moreover, it was noted to the eighty thousand people who received a copy of the pamphlet that the land to produce the crops was readily available to anyone who could get himself to L.A. "This county offers you cheap lands, with a soil capable of producing all crops in abundance and inexhaustible in richness . . . a climate unexcelled in the world."

The Chamber focused on attracting farmers from the Midwest and South, and sent out tens of thousands of its publications. The Chamber also underwrote the publication of the first issues of *Land of Sunshine*. Initially it, too, was a promotional tool, full of ads and articles about Southern California, edited by Charles Dwight Willard, the Chamber's secretary. It was later transformed into a leading journal of the arts and attractions of the Southwest when Charles Fletcher

Harper's magazine introduced the rest of the country to Southern California in its December 1882 issue. The orange groves are near the San Gabriel Mission.

Top right: View of the celery district in Venice. April 12, 1927

Right: Produce carts, common in most American cities in the early twentieth century, appeared in Los Angeles year-round with most of the produce locally grown and picked right off the tree or vine.

Lummis assumed the editorship with the January 1895 issue, eventually changing the name to *Out West* in 1902.

The Chamber was in its third headquarters above the Mott Market on Main Street between First and Second Streets when it first published *The County and City* (later changed to *The City and County*) by Harry Ellington Brook. The first issue of this often updated pamphlet was readied for distribution at the Chicago World's Fair of 1893. A column on the left side of the cover listed products of the County, all of them agricultural except for petroleum and asphaltum. Inside was a lightly-illustrated guide to the towns of Southern California and a lengthy guide to growing various crops. By the end of the Fair, more than fifty thousand free copies had been distributed. Several other promotional brochures Brook wrote for the Chamber also had distribution in the tens of thousands.

Frank Wiggins conceived the idea of displaying the products of the Southland's farms closer to home. In 1893 he leased Henry Hazard's Pavilion at Fifth and Olive and filled the largest exposition space in the city with the bountiful produce of Southern California's farms. The huge crowds of locals and tourists who turned out for the agricultural exposition convinced the Chamber to construct a permanent exhibit space at its Main Street headquarters to display the results of local farms, as well as the minimal

Below: The written note on this postcard of the fifth Chamber headquarters informed a friend in East Boston, "This building contains specimens of all kinds of varieties of California products. Also a fine collection of Indian curios." February 27, 1907

The Chamber of Commerce,
Los Angeles, Cal.

Postcard featuring
the displays inside the
Chamber building
on Broadway.

Top tight: Frank
Wiggins' most famous
creation—the walnut
elephant. Once again,
a Chamber secretary is
drafted into boosting
service.

industrial output of the region. The sixty-by-ninety-foot display area was twenty-two feet high. When the Chamber constructed its fourth headquarters at Broadway and Fourth Streets in 1894 (with its name in bas relief on the Broadway side), it contained an eighty-by-one-hundred-twenty-foot exhibit space on the second floor with a height under the skylight of forty feet. Overhanging galleries offered a view of the generously displayed local produce and manufacturing, along with a walnut elephant.

As bizarre as it sounds, the walnut elephant was the chief attraction at the exhibit. The original design came from Wiggins, the Chamber's director of exhibits. Initially displayed at the Chicago World's Fair in 1893, the elephant was somewhat larger than life size and consisted of a wire grid over a wooden frame, completely covered with fifteen thousand large California walnuts. On its back was a howdah, or seat, with a canopy and railing. As was typical with the perennial Rose Parade in Pasadena and the occasional La Fiesta floral parade in L.A., the howdah was made of home-grown agricultural products: corn, wheat, barley and moss, and was strapped around the elephant by a belt of lemons. The pachyderm became so popular that Wiggins built a mate that traveled the country as part of the Chamber's exhibit at state fairs.

The fifteen-foot-high elephant remained the centerpiece of the Chamber exhibit for thirty years. It was eventually joined by a twelve-foot-high bottle of wine. This did not last as long, being retired in 1919 upon the passage of the Volstead Act abolishing the sale of alcohol. Another transient was the twenty-foot-high ear of corn, which was crafted from forty-five bushels of white Dent corn. Joining the oversized pieces in the Chamber's hall were exhibits on both agricultural and industrial products produced in Southern California. The Chamber also offered a narrated glass slide show, which was eventually replaced by Chamber-generated movies. Lectures on various topics related to visiting or remaining in Los Angeles were held throughout the day. The idea of the Chamber's permanent exhibit was to introduce onlookers to the wonders of Southern California in hopes they would stay. For those who did, there were free lists of real-estate offices and apartment houses in the city. The exhibit hall proved so popular that even the non-Chamber city guides recommended it as the place to start a visit to Los Angeles. Obviously visitors were paying attention. Attendance at the new exhibit hall averaged about a hundred thousand per year, with almost half the visitors coming in during the height of the winter tourist season.

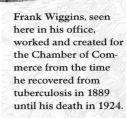

Not even a decade past the crushing end of the "Boom of the '80s," the Chamber took justifiable pride in its initial efforts at boosterism. Charles Dwight Willard, the first secretary of the Chamber, boasted in the *Members Annual for 1894,* "It is generally admitted that Los Angeles is the best advertised city in Southern California, the best advertised section in the Union, and it cannot be questioned that this has resulted in a considerable measure from the persistent work of the Chamber of Commerce." The organization was founded "at a time when the press of the whole country united in abusing this section, and the fortunes of the people were at the lowest ebb."

Frank Wiggins, seen here in his office, worked and created for the Chamber of Commerce from the time he recovered from tuberculosis in 1889 until his death in 1924.

One of the prefabricated sectional Chamber of Commerce exhibits. Des Moines, Iowa, 1934

But this was only the beginning. The tectonic shift in the promotional campaign began when Frank Wiggins was diagnosed with tuberculosis. At the age of fifty-four, Wiggins sold his interest in a family hardware business in Richmond, Indiana, and came to Los Angeles to regain his health or die. He recovered, joined the Chamber of Commerce in 1889 and was made its director of publicity the next year. He came to so completely dominate the organization that the Chamber's own official record noted that "the modern history of Los Angeles and its Chamber of Commerce really began with a man named Frank Wiggins."

After scoring publicity coups with California on Wheels, the Chicago World's Fair and the Chamber's own exhibit area, Wiggins was chosen to succeed Willard as the secretary, or day-to-day leader, of the Chamber of Commerce in 1897. In this position, Wiggins became a Los Angeles legend. What Harris Newmark described as his "fiercely bewhiskered" countenance

"Oranges and snow" was the most ubiquitous image in the entire booster campaign. The scene at right is from a 1909 tourist booklet called *Scenic Beauties of Southern California: The Land of Winter Sunshine, Fruits and Flowers*. It features an artesian well near San Bernardino, noting the "abundant subterranean water supply."

Below: the cover of the Southern Pacific-financed *Sunset* magazine. Unlike *Land of Sunshine/Out West*, which became a serious literary magazine under Charles Lummis, *Sunset* struck an odd balance between boosterism, serious literature, and art and lifestyle.

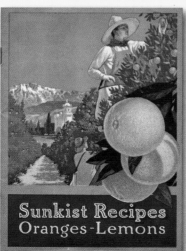

The *Land of Oranges* booklet was meant to introduce children to the growing, processing and consuming of oranges.

Sunkist joined the other booster organizations in celebrating oranges and snow. The recipe booklet on the left is from 1916. The 1930 Pacific Electric pocket guide reflects the lowered booster expectations of the line.

Put Your Name in the Worlds Largest Register

Size
29"long 27"wide 17" thick
Weight 350 lbs.
4000 Pages
108,000 names

Please do not skip spaces

became the living embodiment of the promotional campaign. In his *Collier's* article on the growth of Los Angeles, Peter Clark MacFarlane noted, "Frank Wiggins is near to being the greatest builder of cities since Peter the Great." So enormous was his impact that the legendary water chief William Mulholland jokingly told the *Times* that the only way to stop the growth of Los Angeles was to "kill Frank Wiggins."

One of Wiggins' revolutionary ideas was to design prefabricated exhibitions that could be reassembled onsite at state fairs, trade expositions and human gathering points of all kinds. Once the exhibits were put together, they were filled out with spokespeople hired by the Chamber, thou-

The Chamber always stressed "clean industry." If they sent a photographer to a factory or packing house, both the place and the workers were sanitized when the picture was to be a closeup.

Prior to World War I, Los Angeles was an overwhelmingly agricultural county. As the county seat, L.A. was home to numerous farm-implement businesses.

sands of pieces of free literature, and the agricultural and industrial products of Southern California. The chief players cooperated to make the campaign so successful: Wiggins created the exhibits and arranged for their transportation and assembly by Chamber of Commerce crews, the County Board of Supervisors helped pay for the exhibits, and the railroads defrayed transportation costs and delivered fresh produce.

Ed Griffin was one of the full-time Chamber workers who toured the country setting up the displays. When he started with the Chamber in 1928, there were nine different prefabricated exhibits. They were designed to be screwed together onsite in two hours. The same setup would not be sent to the same place twice in a row. Pamphlets and oil paintings accompanied the local manufacturing and agricultural products on display, and the perishable fruits and vegetables were restocked daily with fresh shipments from home.

All this was prepared and staffed by the Chamber through the Publicity Fund of the Los Angeles County Board of Supervisors. The County money paid the salaries of twenty-five people at the Chamber, including the men who traveled with the sets to county fairs and expositions all over the United States. As the promotional campaign wound down during the Depression, the traveling exhibits appeared only at larger expositions. World War II and the enormous rush of veterans to Los Angeles spelled the end of the traveling exhibits, although they still appeared at the Orange Show in San Bernardino as well as the Ventura and Los Angeles County Fairs until 1955. (When the Chamber moved to its much smaller headquarters on

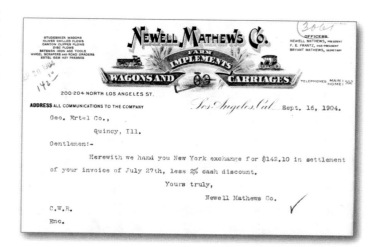

As this is on the roof of the Chamber of Commerce, you can only surmise that once again several secretaries showed up for work and soon found themselves knee deep in walnuts, posing with the Walnut Queen and celebrating the award-winning fourteen-million-dollar walnut crop.

Bixel Street in 1956, the Publicity Fund was discontinued. For the first time since C.D. Willard and Frank Wiggins thought of showing off local products some sixty years before, the Chamber had no exhibit space either on the road or in its headquarters).

Besides overseeing the Chamber's daily activities and orchestrating the booster campaign, Wiggins also wrote several articles and pamphlets. One of his best was *A Few Nuts and How to Crack Them* published in 1915. In *A Few Nuts*, Wiggins explains how to grow walnuts, peanuts and almonds, and what to watch out for in the process. Citing statistics that production had gone from two hundred railroad carloads in 1893 to more than nine hundred in 1911, he writes, "California bids fair to become known as the Land of the English Walnut, as it is already known as the land of the orange and lemon." Wiggins notes that acreage could be bought from eight hundred dollars to twelve hundred dollars and brought to bearing for an additional four hundred dollars to six hundred dollars per acre. He goes on to discuss the type of land needed to grow walnuts, how much water is necessary and how to bring the trees to maturity.

The Chamber sent out such literature by the trainload. In the year from February 1898 to February 1899, 127,000 pieces were distributed in Omaha, Nebraska, alone. An additional twenty-three thousand pieces went to Washington, D.C., for the National Educational Association, and

Sunkist was as convinced as everyone else that a pretty girl sells the picture. Not an average day in the Southland's orange groves.

sixty thousand were picked up at the Chamber's own Exhibit Hall. Thousands of other copies were distributed in the permanent displays the Chamber operated from storefronts in Chicago, Washington, D.C. and Atlantic City. These offices not only gave away all the literature they could, they also provided speakers to any group that wanted one.

Frank Wiggins was always on the lookout to better distribute the Chamber's publications. So when a gold strike in the remote Klondike region of northwestern Canada drew thousands of miners to northern Canada in 1897 and 1898, Wiggins determined that the miners would like to hear about a land of sunshine. So he prepared a special Klondike edition of *Los Angeles City and County,* which was sent out in March. The *Annual Report* noted, "Returns have been received to the effect that many of them were seen in camps in the frozen region, where they were read with much interest." There was no record of how many of the miners brought their broken dreams and frostbitten toes to the land of the palm tree, but the Chamber, as always, was in there pitching.

In 1900, the Orange Carnival in Chicago had a major Los Angeles Chamber-created exhibit which was visited by more than one hundred thousand people. Other displays were at the Midwinter Fair in San Francisco, the Cotton States International Exposition in Atlanta, the Trans-Mississippi and International Exposition in Omaha, as well as a dozen other venues. The Atlantic City storefront alone generated more than four hundred requests for information from the Chamber each week. Pamphlets continued to flow out of the Chamber headquarters: ten thousand copies of the descriptive pamphlet *City and County*; three thousand copies of a chart on the rainfall in Los Angeles; fifteen thousand copies of *Climate and Health.* That same year the Chamber sent out another ten thousand copies of the *Times' Mid-Winter Edition* and had more than a million people see its contribution to the "California on Wheels" traveling exhibit.

It is clear that these pamphlets were not simply being sent off into the ether and ignored. One recipient was Jane Meredith, who lived on a farm near Kirkwood, Iowa. On December 21, 1889 she wrote a very poignant letter to her cousin Lawson, who had moved to Pasadena. She pointed out that she and her two sisters were alone on the farm and wanted to sell the place. As Americans were wont to do, their family had spread out all over the country. Some were in a

nearby town, others moved off to Indiana, Kansas and St. Louis. But it was to the cousin in Southern California she wrote about moving.

Jane's sister, Lydia, had been sent a pamphlet called *Southern California Paradise* and it had given both of them "the California fever." Her initial question, of course, was "is the climate as good as represented?" The book promised it was possible to make six hundred dollars to one thousand dollars per acre in Pasadena. She asked her cousin, "Does thee realize that much from thine? Or is this book a humbug?" She went on to ask very pointed questions about rainfall, irrigation methods, land prices, how much supplies would cost, and, even in 1889, "Have you ever had any earthquakes since you have been there?" She noted she "would like to come out there if it is as nice as this book represents it," and raises the key question, "what kind of a place it would be for three lone farm women to come to." Clearly the answers were to her liking since she sold the farm and moved west the next year.

The Chamber of Commerce may have been the most aggressive of the organizations promoting the agriculture of Los Angeles in the early twentieth century, but it certainly was not alone. Its booster ardor was matched by Sunkist, which was dedicated to finding better ways to profitably sell citrus fruit. As would later be the case with the film industry, Sunkist only advertised the Southland by proxy. Both were only displaying the glories of the region where their products were developed.

The initial organizational meetings for what became known as the Southern California Fruit Growers Exchange, led by P.J. Dreher of Pomona and T.H.B. Chamblin of Riverside, were held at the Chamber of Commerce headquarters at the Mott Building in April and May of 1893. The

Young Frank, managing the Wiggins family hardware business in Richmond, Indiana before tuberculosis drove him to try "the California Cure" in 1886.

Wiggins and several officers of the Chamber of Commerce look through the memorabilia put in the cornerstone of their soon-to-be-abandoned 1903 fifth headquarters on Broadway. 1924

Above left: Soon after he became Chamber Secretary in 1897, Frank was down at the Southern Pacific's Arcade station.

Left: The A. Phimister Proctor bust of Wiggins in the entranceway of the new Chamber Building on Twelfth Street. 1925

plans were approved and a board was appointed on August 29, 1893. The Exchange was established to fight the severely depressed prices for citrus fruit in the 1890s. These were rocky times for U.S. farmers in general, but Southern California citrus growers had the added problem of being twenty-five hundred miles from the major eastern markets. After a decade of sectional exclusivity, the Exchange dropped "Southern" from its name in 1905 and included growers in Northern California's San Joaquin Valley to make it a statewide organization. Soon it adopted "Sunkist" as its trademark brand.

It was under this name that the organization started its first major campaign in the spring of 1908. The target audience, as with much of the Chamber's promotional effort, was the Midwest. Sunkist declared "Orange Week in Iowa." The Southern Pacific reached an agreement with the Exchange to match amounts spent to make Iowa orange-hungry. Under the slogan, "Oranges for Health—California for Wealth," specially-bannered trains, thousands of pieces of literature, lecturers and billboards were let loose in Iowa. The effort was costing Sunkist and the railroads seven thousand dollars, so they carefully monitored the effort. While the country's Exchange business as a whole increased twenty percent, sales in Iowa shot up fifty percent. In September, an ebullient Exchange upped the advertising budget to twenty-five thousand dollars and pasted six million stickers reading "Sunkist Oranges" and another million saying "Sunkist Lemons" on the labels of Exchange shippers.

The Chamber's *Los Angeles County* series of pamphlets described Los Angeles and the various towns in the county. 1925

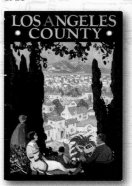

Even though it lost Frank Wiggins in 1924, the Chamber was at the apex of its power and influence when it moved into its new block-long, John Parkinson-designed building in 1925. Fittingly, when the last piece of steel was set in place, the building was christened with a bottle of orange juice. The office block was on Twelfth Street between Broadway and Hill.

Above right: Interior of the Chicago office.

Right: The Chris Siemer mural in the Chamber of Commerce boardroom in the Twelfth Street building.

The Iowa campaign set the style. Sunkist would continue to make the country orange-conscious while it also produced a bucolic, sunny healthy view of Southern California. This was not only done by print advertising and pamphleteering but also by the labels pasted on the orange crates to identify the shipper. The first labels appeared on crates in the 1870s, and grew ever more colorful until they were phased out in the mid-1950s when cardboard boxes replaced wood. During that seventy-year period, Sunkist claimed to have shipped more than two billion crates of oranges with more than eight thousand distinct label designs.

Sunkist successfully shipped its first-quality citrus all over the country by 1915. But there was the problem of poorer-quality fruit. Distributing it would lower the price for the better stuff,

The Patton Ranch was in the west Valley near Owensmouth (now Canoga Park). As the promise of Owens Valley water and new land ownership patterns emerged after 1910, the late nineteenth century wheat fields covering that part of the San Fernando Valley were phased out as dry land farming was replaced by subdivision and truck farming.

but clearly, it was money down the drain to let the lesser citrus go to waste. In 1916, under the slogan "Drink an Orange," Sunkist developed that staple of the American breakfast, orange juice. The campaign was as successful as its Iowa predecessor eight years earlier. After Sunkist invented and marketed a hand juice extractor, consumption of oranges rose from half an orange per serving to two or three. Not surprisingly, lemonade soon followed—lemon sales shot up along with that of oranges. Other producers were quick to pick up on the idea, with juice from tomatoes, grapes, apples and prunes soon being aggressively marketed. By the end of World War I, Sunkist was distributing five hundred million advertisements annually in more than twenty magazines and four hundred daily newspapers.

The orange was the perfect shorthand for the semi-

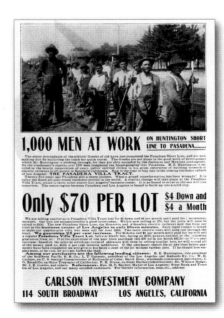

1,000 MEN AT WORK ON HUNTINGTON SHORT LINE TO PASADENA.......

Only $70 PER LOT $4 Down and
$4 a Month

CARLSON INVESTMENT COMPANY
114 SOUTH BROADWAY   LOS ANGELES, CALIFORNIA

Owning your own productive small farm was one of the major selling points in the promotional campaign. Selling those farmers the tools of their trade was one of the first L.A. industries.

Left: Ad that appeared in *Out West* concerning Henry Huntington's new interurban line to Pasadena. As was common prior to World War I, the laying of the track was tied to the development of new tracts.

The Union Wholesale Terminal Market east of Downtown on Alameda. 1925

Loading bursting Sunkist boxes at the harbor.

Right: One of the last agricultural booster pamphlets published by the Chamber in 1928. By then the growth of industry was uppermost in the Chamber's plans. Under the title, "Agriculture—An Industry," the pamphlet explains that the term "encompasses all the economic products of the soil, as well as those industries necessarily dependent on these products. And full definition of agriculture is our birthright in Southern California, for here it has reached greatest development as an industry and a mode of living."

tropical climate and healthy environment the boosters so loudly proclaimed. Though agriculture largely faded from the promotional campaign in the 1920s, citrus fruit grew ever more central to the projected image of the city. The Chamber of Commerce may have stressed industrial growth in its publicity, but it still expressed pride that Los Angeles remained the leading agricultural county in the United States. In one of its last major rurally-themed pamphlets, the Chamber celebrated *Los Angeles: The Center of an Agricultural Empire* (1928), and emphasized that the generous growing season, buttressed by plentiful water for irrigation, ensured that "the effort of the Southern California agriculturalist is shorn of much of the risk and uncertainty which confronts the farmer in other sections of the country." Additionally, a fine road system connected farmers with all the natural attractions of Southern California living, so they were not "deprived of pleasurable living, which has always been considered a necessary complement consequent to successful agriculture."

The promotional campaign would always strive to keep in touch with changes in Los Angeles and the country at large. As the nation urbanized in the 1920s, the Chamber

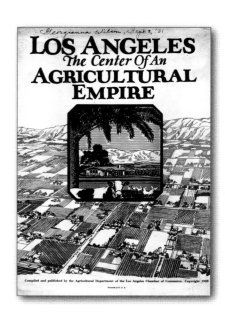

Art Streib was dispatched to the National Orange Show in San Bernardino to take a picture of Dorothy Short in her dress of orange leaves and fruit.

The 1929 *Los Angeles County To-day* pamphlets covered the various towns and cities of the county, as well as topics such as agriculture, industry, commerce, aviation and, of course, climate. In contrast, the 1913 edition pictured a rotund Franciscan friar standing under the arch with a much smaller city and virtually no industry behind him.

Long Beach sales office, representative house, and lots at 899 Willow Street.

Middle row: Manning the Wagner-Thoresen sales office in the wilds of Van Nuys at Sherman Way and Lane Street. February 18, 1926; You might win a new coupe to drive to your lot in the biggest year of the 1920s boom, 1923; Donahue and Handley real-estate office at 322 S. La Brea Avenue, offering lots and houses in Hancock Park, Wilshire Highland Square, Melrose Park and others. July 21, 1925

Bottom row: Luring you to Handy Homes on South Figueroa Street. c. 1923; Boarding the LARY after viewing the new development at Leimert Park. March 24, 1927

would become ever more concerned with the industrialization of Southern California. The emphasis on farming, which had been so central to the early campaign, was gradually eclipsed by a more contemporary concern with industry. The Chamber started promoting climate more as a means to a contented labor force, and less as the ultimate source of "growing conditions to meet the requirements of any phase of agriculture."

Promotional photograph labeled "Los Angeles' Newest Real Estate Subdivision," at Stocker and Crenshaw. The real-estate agent set up sixty-foot arrows to guide people to it.
April 1, 1931

Below: Sheet music, for a place where "orange trees scent the breeze . . . There I'll settle down beneath the palms, in someone's arms, in Pasadena." It was one of Harry Warren's first hits, introduced by Paul Whiteman's orchestra in 1923. He went on to be nominated for eleven Oscars, winning three.

Beverly Hills celebrating what may still be the record for population growth. It went from empty rolling hills in 1920 to the chief home for movie folk and other newly rich people by 1930.

CHAPTER FOUR

Culver City was only thirteen years old when the results of the 1930 census were released. It was most famous as the home of the Metro-Goldwyn-Mayer Studio, which had "more stars than there are in Heaven," but shared in the Southland's elation over population gain.

POPULATION FIGURES

The pure delight that was taken in the enormous population growth of the early twentieth century seems odd now that it has become so miserable driving around the city. But more people meant the boosters were winning and the Southland was becoming the colossus they had envisioned.

The Goodyear plant was constructed on agricultural land at 66th and Central in South Los Angeles. In the photo above, construction is about halfway done and the Ascot Speedway is closed. 1919

GOODYEAR TIRE AND RUBBER

Prior to 1919, the Chamber of Commerce referred to Los Angeles as "B.G."— Before Goodyear. It was the first major eastern manufacturer to open a new facility in the Angel City. Firestone and Goodrich soon followed. A decade later Los Angeles was second only to Akron, Ohio, in rubber-products production.

Los Angeles, the industrial city—the workshop in a garden—puts forth a different appeal than the conventional. Los Angeles, the playground of the nation, is known to the world. Its charms of climate, the call of its beaches and foothills to the vacationist is an oft-told story. But Los Angeles, the manufacturing and distributing center, is a new chord in the hymn of human progress and it seems fitting that some word of explanation should be made.

John Fredericks, President of the Chamber of Commerce,
Southern California Business, 1922

This photo of the oh-so-eastern-looking Post Office at Main and Winston Streets was sold at Rohn's News dealers and Stationers on Spring Street. Selling photographers' work was a common practice in the days before mass-produced postcards and the ubiquitous personal camera.

Like any other small city with ambition in the late nineteenth century, Los Angeles embraced Richardsonian/Romanesque architecture. It was accepted throughout the United States as the guaranteed style to demonstrate seriousness of intent. The City Hall, County Building, Federal Building, high school, and many business blocks were all constructed in the Richardsonian style with its characteristic massive walls. The architecture could not have been less natural for Los Angeles. It was perfectly suited to the east with its miserable weather and well- established social hierarchy, but it looked absurdly thick and overbuilt among the palm trees and sunshine.

The city finally began to exert its own style in the 1920s. Whether in pursuing industries or choosing new architecture, the Chamber was determined to create the city of the future. Los Angeles architects and boosters alike embraced Spanish Colonial Revival, Streamline and Zigzag Moderne, and the just-emerging International Style.

This dedication to modernism paid off when L.A. was illustrated in books and magazines looking so unique and modern. In 1928 *The Independent* ran a photo series on various American cities. St. Louis was full of soot. Duluth was a laborer's city of canals and factories, likewise Kansas City and Cleveland. Los Angeles, by contrast, looked like Oz. The Chamber of Commerce sup-

High School, Los Angeles, Cal

The second, Roman-esque, Los Angeles High School was built on Fort Moore Hill above down-town in 1891. It would last until the third L.A. High was built on Olympic in West Los Angeles in 1917. The Fort Moore site would eventually house a Spanish Revival junior high school and the ever-expanding offices of the Los Angeles Unified School District.

plied all the photos filled with buildings that were gleaming in the sun: City Hall, the Library, the Elks Hall rising out of Westlake Park, Grauman's Chinese Theatre. Then there was more sun—on an old fountain at the San Fernando Mission, on a palm-lined residential street, rising over Easter service at the Hollywood Bowl, and, of course, at the beach. The only industrial photos were of the sanitary interior of an iron mill, of oil derricks surrounded by a huge orange grove and of a studio backlot. For anyone from somewhere else, Los Angeles seemed to exist on a totally different temporal plane than Duluth.

As the twentieth century moved into its second decade, the members of the Chamber of Commerce recognized that if Los Angeles was ever to be the dominant city they envisioned, the Chamber would have to shift its focus. While Duluth was never the model, the Chamber dedicated

One of the most contin-ually booming indus-tries in Los Angeles was construction. As the city hit its stride in the 1920s, even corner markets were Spanish-looking fantasies and dressed up for their premiers. This one is the Slauson View Market at Slauson and Bryanhurst.

**Venice Beach,
January 26, 1931**

itself to making Los Angeles into an industrial city. But it would be a new model for the twenti-eth-century industrial city and would fit with the boosters' vision of the purity of the Southland's environment. They would emphasize "clean" industry. Belching smoke, mountains of slag and toxic water would not characterize the southland's industrial effort. In Chamber-speak, L.A. would be "The Workshop in a Garden."

The Chamber of Commerce took concrete steps toward its new goal in 1915 by creating the Industrial Bureau. Its stated goal was to pursue "our dream of making Los Angeles an impor-tant manufacturing city." Its three aims were to ensure the availability of the raw materials neces-sary for industry, to encourage "home-grown" manufacturing—meaning things that were made in Southern California—and to attract established industry from around the United States. Six years later, the Chamber developed a plan it called the "Balanced Prosperity Fund." The idea was to keep an even pace between the expanding industrial base of the city and the constant population increase. The result would be what the Chamber called "The City of Balanced Progress."

The Chamber already had a quarter-century of experience promoting population increase and agricultural expansion. To achieve its revised goal of rapid expansion of manufacturing, the Industrial Bureau was reconfigured expressly to aid the establishment and expansion of local enterprises. A new Committee on Manufacturers was created to convince established businesses to open branch factories in Los Angeles. All this was aimed at creating the sort of "Balanced Progress" the Chamber referred to, as well as a plethora of products emerging from Southland-based manufacturers.

Throughout the Chamber's push for industrialization, "home-grown products" were boosted as the best choice for local consumers. In one of the earliest pamphlets distributed by the Chamber of Commerce and published by the *Evening Express* in 1891, all the local products discussed were agricultural. By the time the Industrial Bureau was opened twenty-four years later, Los Angeles was twenty-seventh on the list of America's industrial cities. Although a lot of activity was associated with agricultural products, only things such as carriages, furniture and tiles came from Southland manufacturers. To draw attention to what was created locally, the new Industrial Bureau declared a "Home Products Week" barely three months after its founding. From November 1 to November 6, 1915, Los Angeles merchants were urged to display the products of local manufacturers in their windows. The Chamber provided free placards for the occasion, organized and publicized it, sponsored a luncheon with a menu of Southern California products and hosted a "New Industries Night" reception at their headquarters.

This concern for the use of home-grown products would continue throughout the promotional campaign. In 1924 Chamber of Commerce president William Lacy became concerned that New York-based architect Bertram Goodhue was using roofing material from Johns-Manville, also of New York, for the roof of the new Central Library. Lacy voiced his concern at a Chamber of Commerce Board of Directors meeting, noting "Our experience has shown us it is almost invariably the case when an eastern architect is employed . . . like most easterners, he has the belief we are not much of a manufacturing center, and does not give much thought to things manufactured in Los Angeles." Being "wedded to the patronizing of home industry and developing it," Lacy

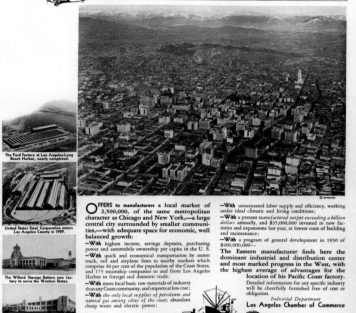

Chamber of Commerce ad touting the new industrial image of the city in *Fortune* magazine, 1930.

Patronize Home Industry!

CALIFORNIA OSTRICH FEATHERS

DIRECT FROM THE

Ostrich Farm at South Pasadena, Cal., which no Tourist should Fail to Visit.

Boas, Capes, Collars, Tips, Amazons and Demi-Plumes.

California Feathers are considered the best on the market. The farm is located between Los Angeles and Pasadena, on electric car line, and is open daily to visitors. **Send for Feather Price List** to

CAWSTON & COCKBURN,
South Pasadena, Cal.

Nearly 100 Birds of all Ages.

Please mention that you "saw it in the LAND OF SUNSHINE."

waged an unsuccessful campaign to have a local manufacturer develop the roof for the Library. Even if the Johns-Manville roof might last longer, the Chamber president wasn't swayed. With a singleness of purpose that was the hallmark of the entire booster campaign, Lacy noted, "We would be perfectly justified in using local roofing because I believe it will last long enough."

The Chamber of Commerce was the loudest and most persistent voice in the effort to industrialize the Los Angeles economy, but it was certainly not alone. The Merchants and Manufacturers Association helped in the preparation of the prospectus books prepared to inform established companies about the opportunities for a branch in the Southland. The railroads were obviously thrilled with the new turn of events and expanded the local track system while making freight rates more attractive. The Los Angeles Realty Board gave its own twist to the Chamber mantra. The Board noted, "The permanent population of Los Angeles need be limited only by our ability to provide newcomers with the means of making a living here. For it seems that almost everybody looks forward to making this favored city his home."

William Mullholland on the banks of the Colorado River in 1925 at Boulder Canyon, the proposed site of the largest dam to be built until that time. It would eventually be repositioned downriver at Black Canyon, though it would retain its original name until it was officially christened Hoover Dam and completed in 1935.

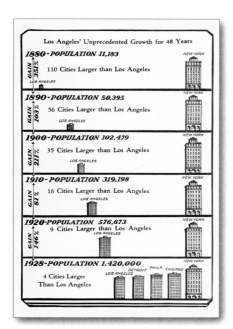

Los Angeles' Unprecedented Growth for 48 Years

1880-POPULATION 11,183
GAIN 351% 110 Cities Larger than Los Angeles

1890-POPULATION 50,395
GAIN 103% 56 Cities Larger than Los Angeles

1900-POPULATION 102,479
GAIN 211% 35 Cities Larger than Los Angeles

1910-POPULATION 319,198
GAIN 81% 16 Cities Larger than Los Angeles

1920-POPULATION 576,673
GAIN 146% 9 Cities Larger than Los Angeles

1928-POPULATION 1,420,000
4 Cities Larger Than Los Angeles

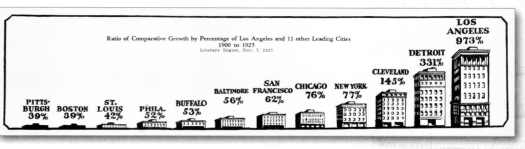

Ratio of Comparative Growth by Percentage of Los Angeles and 11 other Leading Cities
1900 to 1925
Literary Digest, Nov. 7, 1925

LOS ANGELES 973%

DETROIT 331%

CLEVELAND 145%

NEW YORK 77%

CHICAGO 76%

SAN FRANCISCO 62%

BALTIMORE 56%

BUFFALO 53%

PHILA. 52%

ST. LOUIS 42%

BOSTON 39%

PITTS-BURGH 39%

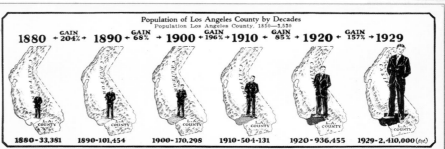

Population of Los Angeles County by Decades
Population Los Angeles County, 1850—3,530

1880 →GAIN 204%→ **1890** →GAIN 68%→ **1900** →GAIN 196%→ **1910** →GAIN 85%→ **1920** →GAIN 157%→ **1929**

1880-33,381   1890-101,454   1900-170,298   1910-504-131   1920-936,455   1929-2,410,000 (Est.)

All this booster interest would have been pointless without a lot of preliminary work that made the creation of an industrial base in Los Angeles possible. The completion of the Owens Valley Aqueduct in November of 1913 made a legend of water chief William Mulholland and provided Los Angeles with both enough water to grow beyond a population of one hundred thousand people and with a surplus of electrical capacity. The city was also well supplied with petroleum resources. Edward Doheny and Charles Canfield drilled the first successful oil well in 1892 on Crown Hill near downtown. Huge strikes would follow at Huntington Beach in 1920 and Santa Fe Springs and Signal Hill in 1921. As important as oil was to the Southland's economy, it was mentioned but never featured in the promotional campaign because it was tough to present as the sort of "clean," non-polluting industry favored by the boosters.

Energy and water supplies were in place, but no matter how much oil and electricity were available, they were useless without the means to ship finished products to distant markets. By the early twentieth century, three transcontinental train lines served Los Angeles—the Salt Lake Railroad (later Union Pacific) having joined the Southern Pacific and Santa Fe—but there was still very poor transportation available by sea. Civic leaders, led, as usual, by the Chamber of Commerce, had been

In 1929 the Meline Real Estate Company published an ornate pamphlet orgasmically celebrating the astounding growth of the city during the 1920s. The theme, of course, is INVEST! The Great Depression would soon start to cool this sort of unbridled booster ardor.

Bottom: Nineteenth-century industry in Los Angeles was never on a massive scale. The loaded delivery carriages are at the Vaughan Box Manufacturer.

As befits the only home-grown major rubber manufacturer, Samson really got into the Hollywood-drenched spirit of things when it built its new factory on Telegraph Road in Commerce.

The main entrance to the office spaces at Goodyear. The tower would have to be demolished following the 1933 Long Beach earthquake.

Where Loyalty to Quality and Home Industry Are One

No doubt it is a matter of pride to every thinking citizen that Los Angeles should be the home of such solidly prosperous manufacturing enterprises as Goodyear.

To us, however, it is a matter of much deeper satisfaction that the product of these factories should always represent a standard of quality not anywhere surpassed. From the day the first Goodyear Tire was made here, the utmost in tire value—design, materials and workmanship—was supplied to Western motorists by this wholly Western factory.

Your preference for Goodyear Tires is a natural preference for the West and the best.

GOODYEAR
"Los Angeles Made For Western Trade"

In an ad published in *Southern California Business* in year four of the Goodyear era, the company covered both the issue of product quality and the old Los Angeles concern about the preference for local products.

Right: It went without saying that Goodyear would have one of the premier booths at the Monroe Centennial Exposition that was set up in Exposition Park from July 24 to August 5, 1923.

The tale of two harbors. On the left is a tourist photo of the Long Wharf at Santa Monica. The Southern Pacific tracks that fed it are in the foreground. The large structure on the pier is a coal bunker. The sign at the entrance demands "Smoking is not permitted on this wharf."

pushing the federal government for funds to improve the San Pedro anchorage and roadway since the 1890s. Clearly, if Los Angeles was to be more than an agricultural center and tourist resort, it needed a dependable deep-water harbor.

Originally, Los Angeles was a land-locked city. The traditional harbor for the small town was twenty miles away at San Pedro and Wilmington. Besides the distance, other problems with the harbor involved mudflats, salt marshes and a very pesky sandbar. It was not a deep-water, protected anchorage like San Diego, San Francisco, Oakland or Seattle. Ocean-going ships were unable to pull up to a pier. Rather, they had to anchor offshore and transfer cargo by smaller vessels with minimal draft, called lighters, a time-consuming and expensive operation.

The Chamber of Commerce, Army Corps of Engineers and anyone who could read a map thought the obvious site for a harbor in the Los Angeles area was San Pedro. It was neatly tucked into the southwest-facing bulk of Palos Verdes and the San Pedro Hills. It was also served by the Southern Pacific, Santa Fe and Los Angeles Terminal railroads. Therein lay the rub. In 1893, in a gesture staggering in its cosmic selfishness, San Francisco-based Collis P. Huntington, designated the Long Wharf north of Santa Monica that was monopolized by his Southern Pacific Railroad to be "Port Los Angeles." He then strenuously lobbied Congress to have his 4,720-foot-long pier, not San Pedro, become the official port of the city.

The Chamber invariably referred to its preferred site as a "free harbor" since it would not be dominated by the Southern Pacific or any other entity. Desiring to avoid "entangling agreements of any kind" on a harbor whose "control should be unconditional and unqualified," the Chamber also refused any money from the commercial bodies of San Francisco or from the State of California.

This pamphlet is an invitation to a Chamber of Commerce "smoker" with no such restrictions for the night of July 13, 1913. This was understood to be a men's gathering to discuss something, in this case the work at San Pedro. Women at that time were not expected to sully their lungs with the devil's weed.

The majestic coastal steamer *Harvard* heads up the Main Channel on its way to San Francisco. It will soon pass Globe Mills grain elevators holding the thousands of tons of wheat that had been harvested in the San Fernando Valley and the Los Angeles plain. March 18, 1923

Right: This wire service photograph was released to celebrate "Foreign Trade Week" in 1927. The Wide World agency got in the spirit of the booster movement by noting of San Pedro that its "phenomenal growth is one of the wonders of the age." Of particular note are the piles of lumber being delivered to Los Angeles. One of the reasons the city needed a harbor was to have a place where all the imported lumber used in building the hundreds of thousands of homes and apartments could land.

The official "programme" of the opening ceremonies of the new harbor. The cover illustration might also be taken to be read as the booster's view of the dynamic twentieth-century Los Angeles overtaking the somnolent early nineteenth-century city.

The perceived nature of the Southern Pacific as a corporate octopus that wanted utter dominance in California was a key argument employed by all San Pedro harbor supporters. The fight for the San Pedro site was long and bitter, but ultimately successful. The first rock in what was to become the largest man-made harbor in the United States was dumped off Point Fermin on April 26, 1899, when President William McKinley pressed a button in Washington—an early media moment. The massive breakwater was finally completed in 1910. Four years later, ships began arriving at San Pedro via the newly opened Panama Canal. As for the Long Wharf in Santa Monica, the depot, coal bunker and one-third of the almost five-thousand-foot-long pier was dismantled in 1913. The rest was demolished in 1920. Thirteen years later, the Pacific Electric abandoned its run to Santa Monica Canyon.

Once the question of where the harbor would be located was answered, the question of civic control had to be addressed. As the new century dawned, San Pedro and Wilmington were independent towns. In order to keep control of its harbor, Los Angeles annexed a one-mile-wide, sixteen-mile-long "Shoestring Addition" to connect the harbor towns. This made for an oddly shaped city, but by California law, communities had to be contiguous. It was still up to the citizens of Wilmington and San Pedro whether they wanted to relinquish their independence. Los Angeles offered a sweet deal. In exchange for annexation, the city would spend more than ten million dol-

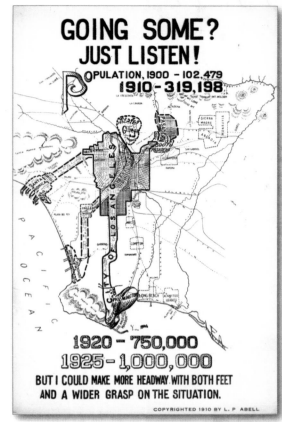

This Chamber of Commerce letterhead made it evident how proud they were of the new harbor. All that smoke rising from hoped-for factories in the background demonstrates what was believed to be in store.

lars in harbor improvements over ten years, build schools, fire and police stations and a ferry route, as well as provide the all-important water from the Owens Valley Aqueduct. The vote passed. President Howard Taft was on hand at the formal annexation ceremonies on August 28, 1909.

Now that the city had a dependable harbor to support its plentiful supplies of oil, water and electricity, the Chamber's Committee on Manufacturers, supported by the Merchants and Manufacturers Association and representing the Los Angeles County Board of Supervisors, was able to lead a successful fight to persuade Goodyear Tire and Rubber executives to choose Los Angeles as the site for the company's West Coast plant. Chamber representatives visited the Goodyear board at the original factory in Akron, Ohio, and presented the company with a prospectus book that was an odd combination of promotion and fact. Growth rates and sunshine levels were noted. The quality of the labor force, weakness of unions, and availability of housing and inexpensive land were all discussed. The pitch was successful. Goodyear built its plant in a cauliflower field near the Ascot Speedway in south Los Angeles at 66th and Central. By the end of the next decade, Goodrich and Firestone joined with homegrown Samson Tire and Rubber and Goodyear to make Los Angeles second only to Akron as the largest rubber-producing city in the United States.

The Samson Company certainly got into the spirit of the promotional campaign. In 1918 its first factory on Fifth Street, like the Goodyear factory on Central Avenue, was a standard-issue brick-and-skylight box. The 1929 factory was more in keeping with a city where anything was

In the early twentieth century, Henry Huntington pushed new streetcar lines into country he intended to develop. By the 1920s, it was the automobile that led to the new lots. Many of the new additions came to the city due to small towns such as Sawtelle and Hollywood that wanted to be connected to Owens Valley water.

The new Spanish Revival Goodrich plant, surrounded by open parkland in April, 1927. Immediately to its north side, wheat was still being harvested as the tires started rolling off the line. The equally new Willard Storage Battery factory is just south of Goodrich on Olympic Boulevard in East Los Angeles.

Top right: Harvey Firestone—assisted by his sons Russel, Leonard and Harvey, Jr.—pulls the first tire off his Los Angeles assembly line on June 21, 1928. It would later be presented at a Chamber of Commerce conference at the Biltmore.

possible. The interior was the typical factory layout, but the exterior was designed to suggest an Assyrian palace, replete with bas-relief figures carved on the walls. The Chamber often pictured the exterior of Samson in its publications. Describing the new, fortress-like factory, the Chamber noted, "Here the eye for business had not closed for beauty." Not as adventurous as Samson was, Goodrich and Firestone celebrated local traditions by designing Spanish Revival factories.

Related to the tire and rubber manufacturers was another former monopoly of the Great Lakes region, the automobile industry. In a 1937 publication called straightforwardly, *Pictures of Industrial Plants,* the Chamber of Commerce illustrated why Los Angeles was the "Automobile Assembly Center of the West." Ford, General Motors (Buick, Oldsmobile and Pontiac divisions), Willys-Overland, Studebaker, Nash and Chrysler plants were illustrated, with Chevrolet, Kaiser and Lincoln-Mercury on the way. Besides the access to Asian and Pacific Coast markets offered through the Port of Los Angeles, part of the appeal of Southern California to auto manufacturers was that the Southland populace was so rabid for their products. In 1929, the United States average was one auto for every 5.13 persons. In L.A. it was one for every 3.2 people. Los Angeles had more cars per capita than any city in the world, and the largest, most active Automobile Club in the country. Los Angeles envisioned itself as the home to all that was new and modern. Cars were a huge part of that.

Population growth was celebrated in many ways in the Southland. The cartoon below appeared in the 1911 *Los Angeles Times* Mid-Winter edition. The one on the right is from *Southern California Business* in July 1930.

Los Angeles Population 1,231,730

Below: This was one of the letter-heads used by booster deluxe and downtown developer William Garland. It is interesting to note the psychic proximity of the harbor and the early twentieth century view of belching smoke-stacks as representing prosperity.

Climate was always the major selling point for any ot the booster groups in any promotional situation. The cartoon above is from the February 26, 1925 issue of *Life*.

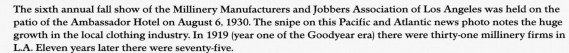

The sixth annual fall show of the Millinery Manufacturers and Jobbers Association of Los Angeles was held on the patio of the Ambassador Hotel on August 6, 1930. The snipe on this Pacific and Atlantic news photo notes the huge growth in the local clothing industry. In 1919 (year one of the Goodyear era) there were thirty-one millinery firms in L.A. Eleven years later there were seventy-five.

The brand-new Ford Motor plant on the Long Beach side of the Badger Avenue bascule drawbridge along the Cerritos Channel. It replaced a multistoried factory located downtown. 1930

Rubber was not only used for tires in sunny SoCal. Even though football season is a long way off, the Associated Press has a group of "bathing beauties" practicing at the beach. The ten-foot-long ball was actually built for a push-ball game.

The industrial promoters agreed upon the benefit of a Central Manufacturing District. The idea of concentrating industries had proved very successful in Chicago. In 1923 the Chamber successfully persuaded the directors of the Chicago CMD to invest in an L.A. counterpart in the Vernon district. Besides the dozens of new industries, a major feature of the district would be the Los Angeles Junction Railway. It was an independent belt line dedicated to moving the cars of the Southern Pacific, Santa Fe, Union Pacific, and Pacific Electric railroads around in the district and south to the Harbor. The various train yards of the city could accommodate 25,518 rail cars. A junction railway could move the enormous number of cars from several different railroads quickly and economically. There were one hundred twenty-five lots in the district, all served by the belt line and connected to the main lines of the four major carriers. When it was up and running, the CMD featured manufacturing companies, distribution outlets and a major cattle yard.

One of the great lures to draw industry to Los Angeles in the early twentieth century was the promoters' claim that the city was "the home of contented labor." Unlike San Francisco, they boomed, L.A. was one of the leaders in the anti-union movement. They stressed the "open," or non-union, shop. The workers who relocated to Los Angeles brought with them all their skills, but in Chamber parlance, were willing to leave behind their "old associations," knowing they were coming to an open-shop town. The *Los Angeles Times* had always been a local leader in the fight for what General Otis called, "True Industrial Freedom." The Chamber saw the anti-union stance as one of the best

selling points of industrial Los Angeles. The Merchants and Manufacturers Association was also fervent in its wish to celebrate those who supported the open shop and to condemn and chastise those who did not.

In the Chamber view, besides not having unions to agitate and confuse them, Southern California laborers had other qualities to recommend them to prospective employers. The Chamber took great pains to point out that most California labor was of "native stock" or "the best American types," as opposed to the immigrants who populated most eastern factories. Workers also had the luxury of living in their own homes. The bungalows were small, to be sure, but they were definitely not the grim, overcrowded, virulently unhealthy, anonymous tenements of the East. In fact, the Chamber enthused to prospective L.A. industrialists, "to one accustomed to conditions in the East, the bright and cheery faces of the workers in a Southern California factory are indeed a revelation. The only 'labor problem' in Southern California is to furnish employment to the many who seek it."

This was part of the evidence that Los Angeles was

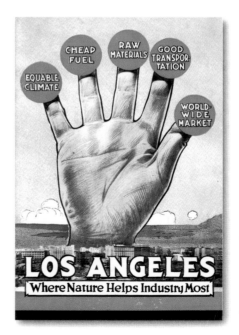

The Los Angeles Union Terminal and Wholesale Terminal on Alameda, proudly trumpeted as the "Largest Group of Warehouses in the West," fills the center of this photo of the heavily-tracked industrial district between the river and downtown.

Above right: The Chamber of Commerce immediately started advertising in the inaugural issue of *Business Week*. September 7, 1929

Left: The main Chamber of Commerce selling points in the concentrated effort to get industries to either relocate or open branch factories in Los Angeles.

the place "Where Nature Helps Industry Most," as the Chamber message shouted. When a local worker was done with his day's work, he not only had no union meeting to attend, he retired to his own home with a backyard and its cool, embracing evening air. Workers found none of the enervating humidity of other manufacturing cities and any number of year-round outdoor activities to keep workers healthy. In *Facts About Industrial Los Angeles,* the Chamber contended, "There is pride of ownership and industrial productiveness in the breasts of the Los Angeles worker, for here he finds the mecca of his hopes and ambitions, contentment for his family and living conditions infinitely better than he could secure anywhere else."

Climate was always the chief selling point about Los Angeles and it was certainly worked into the effort to attract established industry. In a perfect example of a hard-headed businessman being seduced by the arguments of the boosters, Willis Owen, the industrial advisor to financier E.H. Harriman, looked at the balmy air from a business standpoint. Writing in Edward Dickson's progressive *Los Angeles Evening Express,* he noted that climate impacted the company's bottom line: a factory building costing one hundred thousand dollars in the East would only be sixty-two thousand dollars in L.A. Heating, cooling, and ventilation were one-fifth the cost in the Southland. The Southern California worker produced twenty-six percent more at the same wage than his beleaguered eastern counterpart. According to Owen, there were other savings as well:

> It is proven also, because of your climate, that your power rates, local and Panama Canal freight rates, overhead and operating expenses, manufacturing cost and general upkeep are lower here than in the East. Climate costs money or saves money—take your choice.

The use of abundant electric power instead of coal led to a "smokeless, sootless, dirtless factory atmosphere," a dramatic improvement over eastern factories. Echoing the Chamber message of "clean" industry, Owen asked, "Did you ever live in the noted factory city of Pittsburgh, the city where you shovel snow out of your path five months in the year and smoke, soot and dirt off of your face for twelve months in the year?"

Clean, modern industries were what the Chamber coveted most. The boosters often pointed out that Los Angeles was the first American city to be powered exclusively by electricity rather than soot-laden coal. L.A. was not only presented as the fastest-growing city in America, but also the most modern. As the Roaring Twenties came to a close, the boosters could look with pride on the city they created. In fifty years, Los Angeles had gone from being the beleaguered queen of the drought-ridden cow counties to the fifth most populous city in the United States. In the fourteen years since the start of the Industrial Bureau, the city moved up the U. S. Census list of manufacturing cities from a dismal twenty-seventh to an astonishing eighth, all this while still maintaining its standing as the leading agricultural county in the country and the undisputed leader in the tuna canning industry. The mudflats of San Pedro had become second only to New York as the busiest harbor in the nation. Los Angeles was second only to Akron in rubber production and to Detroit in automobile manufacturing. The city led the country in filmmaking and was a significant contributor to oil production, radio entertainment, construction, furniture manufacturing and the design and manufacture of airplanes. Los Angeles also was a leader in the manufacture of the equipment used in the production of movies, airplanes and automobiles. Frank Wiggins summed it up best when he wrote in 1922, "A generation ago we invited attention—now we command it." There has been no other story quite like it in our national history.

The Los Angeles Can Company's float for the La Fiesta Parade made sure to push the fact that it was a home industry. c. 1903

In year two of the Goodyear era, the Chamber displayed its pride in industry in its float in the Tournament of Roses Parade.

CHAPTER FIVE

The Circular Bridge on Mount Lowe, halfway between Echo Mountain and the Alpine Tavern. The crazy bend around the corner of the mountain was simply a way to gain altitude. G.B. McClellan and the other photographers often took pictures of the cars full of happy visitors, seemingly hanging in space on the bridge.

MOUNT LOWE

Thaddeus Lowe and David McPherson. A practical dreamer and a talented engineer. Together they built "The Greatest Mountain Adventure in the World" above Pasadena. The mountain still bears Professor Lowe's name but he was forced to sell the railroad in 1899. Pacific Electric acquired it in 1902 and ran the Alpine Division until nature destroyed it in 1935, shortly after the promotional campaign petered out. But while it was up and running, "The Railway in the Clouds" provided middle- and working-class people a chance to get out of the city to relax or hike as they saw fit.

The Big Red Cars were also a way to get to work or go shopping, such as at the Helms Bakery stop on the Venice Shortline. c. 1934

ON THE TOURIST ITINERARY

There were mandatory stops on the tourist trail, relentlessly advertised by every booster group there was. Judging from the tourist photos that still exist, alligators, ostriches and South Seas islands just off the coast grabbed newcomers' imaginations and made them turn to the "Wizardry of Kodakery."

Los Angeles is what it is because these folks are what they are; and they're what and where they are because of this same cardinal carrier that wipes distance out of the consideration in a way you never saw anywhere else . . . They enjoy all the conveniences of the city and all the fun of the country. . . . You haven't bumped into anything of this sort because it doesn't exist anywhere else. Los Angeles is the center and heart of the most highly developed interurban electric system in the whole world.

Former Iowan, quoted in "The Red Car of Empire" by Rufus Steele, *Sunset,* October 1913

It's the red cars of the Pacific Electric that everyone thinks of when conjuring up a vision of streetcars on L.A.'s streets. The yellow cars of the Los Angeles Railway do not occupy the high plain in the nostalgia for an older Los Angeles. LARY ran within the city limits of Los Angeles and had generally smaller, more utilitarian cars. They took people to work or shopping, or maybe to see a pal. 1928

Los Angeles has always been a city of great distances. It was a deliberate choice on the part of early leaders of the city to keep it horizontal rather than vertical. This alleviated the problems of crowding inherent in large cities everywhere, but it also led to serious questions about moving goods and people across the Southland. The situation was exacerbated by the astonishing growth in population and tourism. Transportation would turn out to be as vital to the promotional campaign as establishing an industrial base.

One solution to this dilemma was an extensive trolley system that grew as haphazardly as the city it served. It eventually coalesced into two major systems, the Los Angeles Railway (LARY or Yellow Cars) and the fabled Pacific Electric (P.E. or Red Cars). By 1929 the LARY system ran within the city limits of Los Angeles on 406 miles of track while the Pacific Electric was the largest interurban system in the world, with 1,164 miles of track at its apex, connecting the far-flung parts of the city as well as the entire Los Angeles basin.

Though their names, colors and missions were different, both systems were at various times run and developed by Henry E. Huntington, one of the leading boosters and land speculators in the Southland and nephew to Collis P. Huntington, director of the Southern Pacific Railroad. Both companies' existing lines, along with the excursion line to the resort on nearby Mount Lowe and a new route to Long Beach, became part of the Pacific Electric when its articles of incorporation were published on October 29, 1901. This coalescing of lines was the result of Henry Huntington losing the presidency of the Southern Pacific Railroad to financier E.H. Harriman following Collis Huntington's death. With his national aspirations thwarted, Henry Huntington turned his attention to the trolley systems in Southern California.

The great Henry Huntington. His longest-lasting contribution to the Southland is his magnificent museum and library. In his lifetime he also left an indelible mark on the area. His triumvirate of electricity, transportation and land development was key to expanding Southern California. At the height of his wealth and power, he sold off the Pacific Electric to the Southern Pacific Railroad and put most of his enormous energies into expanding his book and art collections. No one was a firmer believer in Andrew Carnegie's "Gospel of Wealth" than Huntington. It was not enough for a man to accumulate a great fortune and just eat very well. It was imperative that he spread it among the citizenry in a way that would do them some good. His railway is long gone, but his library is closing in on a century of service to scholars of all sorts.

Right: In a nice tie-in of booster groups, you could visit the All Year Club's headquarters and then hop on the LARY to see what struck your fancy.

Prior to the automobile revolution of the 1920s, Red Cars were the most popular means of travel about the Southland. Motorman G. H. Mall wrote on the back, "Hooper Avenue Car Line. I sure had a load. Conductors did not get one-fourth of their fares in the year of 1912."

Seven years later, the Pacific Electric had either purchased existing systems or laid new track to include Riverside, Redlands, San Pedro and Orange County in the system. Lines also extended to Huntington's own developments at Alhambra, the San Fernando Valley, Olinda and Pacific City (the town had aptly been renamed Huntington Beach). The line changed again when the Pacific Electric, Los Angeles Railway and seven other Southern California trolley lines were acquired by the Southern Pacific Railroad on August 24, 1911, in what was called "The Great Merger," freeing Henry Huntington to devote more time to his magnificent book and art collections. The expanded Pacific Electric also increased its efforts to promote the allure of Southern California to visitors and potential settlers.

With or without Huntington at the reins, the Pacific Electric played two key roles in the promotional campaign. The first was building streetcar lines in advance of development. This enabled developers to keep expanding outward from central Los Angeles while ensuring that settlers would still be connected with the major job, entertainment and retail

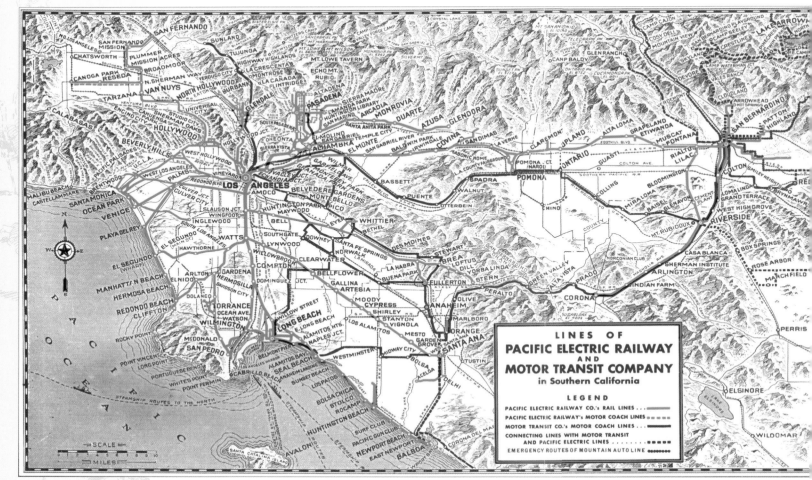

The Red Car lines at their apex in 1934. Ridership was already dropping due to the ever-increasing attachment on the part of Angelenos to their automobiles, and buses were starting to vie with the streetcars. It is evident from the map why the Pacific Electric was so key to early promotion. You could go practically anywhere on it.

district. And second, the P.E.'s own pamphlets and brochures served as an additional means of publicizing the system—particularly its specialized excursions.

Most of the excursion routes had largely been developed by previous trolley companies. From the turn of the century, the extensive trips served to introduce both tourists and prospective settlers to the varied pleasures of Southern California. Several routes came and went over the years, but the three longest survivors visited the most unique spots in the "Climatic Capital of the World." They were the Balloon Route, the Orange Empire Trolley Trip and the Mission Route.

All started at the Pacific Electric Building at Sixth and Main. The Balloon Route went out to the beach cities, stopping for lunch at the Playa del Rey Pavilion and visiting the National Soldiers' Home or Redondo Hotel for a photo op. The Orange Empire Trolley Trip covered San Bernardino, Riverside and Redlands, with a stop at the Mission Inn for lunch and a group photo.

Los Angeles wasn't the only town engaged in promoting paradise. Here are examples from Alhambra (1930), Glendora (c. 1928) and San Bernardino County (1928).

The Pacific Sightseeing Company offered three trips by autobus—to Pasadena and Busch Gardens and the animal farms; Hollywood and Universal City; and the beaches, including Venice, Ocean Park and Santa Monica.

The Mission Route hit San Gabriel, Pasadena and Monrovia; its photo spot was Mission San Gabriel. As the Pacific Electric grew, the Triangle Trolley Trip was added, heading south to San Pedro, then east to Long Beach and Santa Ana, with photos taken at that small town's city hall.

These trolley tours were only part of the Pacific Electric's role in Los Angeles tourism. Visitors were always encouraged to ride the Red Cars to the various tourist venues mentioned in all the guidebooks and promotional literature. While Disneyland and Knott's Berry Farm weren't even close to the drawing board, thanks to the Red Cars tourists flocked to the likes of Selig Zoo, Alligator Farm and Ostrich Farm in Lincoln Heights opposite Eastlake (later Lincoln) Park, Cawston's Ostrich Farm in South Pasadena and Gay's Lion Farm in Pomona. These hot spots shared the theme central to the promotional campaign: Los Angeles is a unique place, full of amazing things you will never see at home, all happening under the best climatic conditions in the United States.

The Selig Zoo is a perfect example. Colonel William Selig needed more land to make movies than his Mission Studio on Alessandro Street in Edendale could provide. So he bought thirty-two acres across the street from tranquil Eastlake Park where the Pacific Electric had been operating an Indian Village to attract visitors to northeast Los Angeles. In 1914 he opened the new studio with his Selig Zoo attached. It featured a very ornate facade with animal figures carved by Italian sculptor Carlo Romanelli. Its seven hundred animals dwarfed the small city zoo (which had just moved to Griffith Park in 1913). Selig, showman extraordinaire, offered the perfect L.A. twist by selling tickets to his zoo plus tours of a *real* movie studio.

Christine Sterling managed to realize her dream of saving Olvera Street and making it a living memorial to early Los Angeles. It was one of the LARY's most popular stops and was featured in this ad. 1928

The Los Angeles Monkey Farm was one of the many attractions offered by Culver City. Like most of the various animal farms scattered about the Southland, the tenants of the Monkey Farm often were seen on movie screens all over the country. The snipe on this Art Streib photo for the *Los Angeles Record* assures viewers that the Pontiac Six roadster pictured is "a favorite with foreign buyers," as evidenced by Roughneck, a native of Africa. April, 1929

By the early 1930s, you could ride all over the Southland for one minimal fare. The big excursion tours were gone by this time, but this pamphlet explains how you could use trolleys and buses to see the sights formerly found on the Orange Empire Route.

Center: The trip down Beverly (later Sunset) Boulevard promised to take you past the new UCLA, Bernheimer's Pacific Palisades gardens, to the Pacific at Castellamare—all by bus. c. 1933

Right: "From the mountains to the sea," as local newscaster Jerry Dunphy used to say. The Pacific Electric had the same idea in this 1915 pamphlet.

The Pacific Electric both served and advertised the other Southland animal farms of the early twentieth century. As noted, the California Alligator Farm and the Los Angeles Ostrich Farm were on Mission Road with the Selig Zoo and Eastlake Park. A visitor had to go to South Pasadena to see Cawston's Ostrich Farm. Gay's Lion Farm was in El Monte, as the brochures liked to say, "only fourteen miles from Seventh and Broadway." Virtually every travel guide of the time noted both the glory and uniqueness of the farms and the fact that the Pacific Electric and LARY provided the best, most efficient means to get there.

A pageful of the Southland's most popular attractions. Gay's Lion Farm in El Monte was the brainchild of Charles and Muriel Gay, veterans of French circuses. Cawston Ostrich Farm in South Pasadena urged visitors to "Co-operate with the government and Audubon Societies for the protection of our wild birds and wear ostrich plumage."

Bottom left: Thanks to the Great White Steamships, Santa Catalina did seem like a true ocean voyage. The Casino building took the place of the Sugar Loaf rock formation and a smaller, octagonal casino that lasted from 1920 to 1928. It has been the signature structure of Avalon ever since.

Longer trips than the Lion Farm were also part of the Red Car kingdom. The two hour and fifteen minute trip to the Mission Inn in Riverside was one of the chief attractions in the entire Southland. The Catalina Special left the P.E. headquarters for the one hour and fifteen minute trip to the terminal at San Pedro to board the *S.S. Cabrillo,* and after 1924, the "Great White Steamship"— the *S.S. Catalina*– or her fellow traveler, the *S.S. Avalon.* The Wrigley Company owned the island and came up with the great promotional tag line "A Trip Like No Other" to describe a visit to Catalina.

Every group that in any way promoted visiting Southern

The Alligator Farm was across the street from Eastlake (later Lincoln) Park, and right next door to the Los Angeles Ostrich Farm.

Charlie Chaplin's house in the Hollywood Hills.

Below: An everyday occurrence at the Alligator Farm. The reins are attached to a muzzle. 1922

Any of the local beaches were major tourist attractions. This is Long Beach, August, 1920.

Left: Both Cawston and Los Angeles Ostrich Farms had a photographer on site to produce a photo postcard to have as a souvenir.

Abbot Kinney's Venice of America, on L.A.'s birthday, September 4, 1912.

Left: Muriel Gay with lion cubs at Gay's Lion Farm, El Monte.

One of the cool nights that visitors were always warned about. On the grand circular balcony of the Casino ballroom on Catalina.

Catalina Island is 22 miles long and 7½ miles wide at Long Point; ¼ mile wide at the Isthmus. It comprises 55,000 acres and is in Los Angeles County, California.

It's not just booster hyperbole. Ever since George Shatto first had the idea to make Catalina accessible to the landlocked masses yearning to breath the lushly scented island air, it has been the Magic Isle. When South Dakota was virtually denuded of buffalo, you could find them on Catalina. Square rigged sailing ships still visited the island for movie work long after they had disappeared from the harbors of the world. The pamphlet this map was in featured an illustration of the new Casino building on the back which was lauded as a "Two Million Dollar Palace of Pleasure for Your Enjoyment."

Below: Sugar Loaf, with its wooden ladder to the top. Consider it a picture of the world prior to the proliferation of law schools.

The most luxurious way to travel to San Francisco and San Diego was via the Collegiate Coastal Twins, the *Harvard* and *Yale*. Like most people and things in early-twentieth-century Los Angeles, they were an import from the East, entering California service in 1908. The Los Angeles Steamship Company was created after World War I at the behest of the Chamber of Commerce to take advantage of the city's gateway to the Hawaiian Islands. Two converted German liners bought from the United States government, which took them as World War I reparations, served the Los Angeles-to-Honolulu route. c. 1924

California urged a visit to Catalina and noted the special Pacific Electric cars. The only Channel Island both open to the public and with facilities for vacationing mainlanders, Catalina was a desirable destination. Since Hawaii was available only by ocean-going steamers, Catalina was the closest most middle- and working-class Americans could come to an island vacation in western America. Every effort was made to enhance the illusion. Palm trees were liberally planted around the town of Avalon, kids dove for coins tossed in the harbor from the visiting steamships, and glass-bottomed boats slowly plied the island's coves to look through the pristine water at the ocean's plant and fish life.

The Catalina Terminal was not the only special destination for Red Cars at the harbor.

San Pedro was one of the ports of call for the *U.S.S. Constitution*, "Old Ironsides," on its trip around the country in March 1933. As always, the Pacific Electric laid on special cars to take the crowds down to the harbor to see the great ship.

Right: The Yale's menu also served as note paper to let a pal know how the trip was going.

Tourist photo of a woman who seems to have chosen her hat as an homage to the Sugar Loaf rocks. 1910

Express cars also left the station at Sixth and Main bound for the berth of the "Collegiate Coastal Twins," the *S.S. Harvard* and *S.S. Yale.* As might be guessed from their names, the two ships were built on the east coast for the Metropolitan Line of New York to use on its overnight run to Boston. They were sold to the Pacific Navigation Company and sailed around Cape Horn to tie up at San Pedro on December 20, 1910. An eighteen-hour run to San Francisco was immediately inaugurated. A biweekly cruise to San Diego was added March 3, 1911. In the years before America's entry into World War I, the *Harvard* and *Yale* were the most luxurious ways for the average person to travel between San Diego, Los Angeles and San Francisco. After the twins did their wartime service ferrying troops to France from England, they were purchased in 1920 by a group formed by the Chamber of Commerce that created the Los Angeles Steamship Company. LASSCO operated the *Harvard* and *Yale,* but was formed to expand the Port of Los Angeles by establishing service from San Pedro to Hawaii.

So key were the trolleys to transportation in the South-

land that all of the major sports and cultural venues built prior to World War II relied on them to deliver the bulk of their attendees. The Memorial Coliseum originally opened in 1923 with room for seventy-six thousand fans, but its architect, the ubiquitous John Parkinson, allowed for expansion to 101,000 should Los Angeles be awarded the 1932 Olympic Games. The Coliseum and the surrounding Exposition Park with its museums, rose garden and picnic areas, was served by six different LARY lines.

Trolley cars were also the chief means of reaching Wrigley Field in South Los Angeles, which had parking for only seven hundred fifty cars. Home to the Los Angeles Angels (and from 1926 to 1935, the Hollywood Stars) of the Pacific Coast League, Wrigley opened in 1925 at 42nd and Avalon and was the one Coast League stadium with a concrete, roof-protected, double-tiered grandstand. It may have been one of the finest minor league parks in the country, but while the PCL was among the highest minor leagues, it was not the majors. So Wrigley Field was noted, but not featured, in the booster campaign.

The Hollywood Bowl was a must-see for tourists and locals alike. The Coliseum, Wrigley Field and Pan-Pacific Auditorium were major sports venues of their time and fit in with the proselytizing about the great and lasting health benefits provided by the outdoor, sports-oriented Southland lifestyle. But the Hollywood Bowl was an outdoor venue that featured great art under the stars in the nation's most perfect climate, so it fit the tenor of the promotional campaign perfectly. While the stadiums were mentioned frequently by the boosters, the Bowl was used as a symbol of artistic accomplishment.

Wrigley Field at 42nd and Avalon in South Los Angeles. The finest ball-park in the Pacific Coast League, which was often referred to as the third major league due to the quality of play. In the photo, Wrigley is being used for the "All Nations Expansion" Assembly in August, 1947. It was also the site of boxing matches, Negro League games, political conventions and Hollywood movies. The lack of parking is evident from the picture. It was every bit as hemmed in by a growing city as Wrigley Field in Chicago or Ebbetts Field in Brooklyn.

Bottom: Catholic mass at the pre-shell Hollywood Bowl. c. 1925

The crown in the P.E.'s excursion program was Mount Lowe—the "Greatest Mountain Adventure in the World." The trolley line that scaled the mountain was the brainchild of Professor Thaddeus Lowe, who, in 1890, hired engineer David Macpherson to design and build a trolley that would leave Rubio Canyon in Altadena, go straight up to 3500-foot Echo Mountain and then up to Ye Alpine Tavern at more than five thousand feet. "The world's greatest mountain railroad" opened for business on the Fourth of July in 1893. In 1902, when economic setbacks forced Professor Lowe to sell his interest in his creation, Pacific Electric took control of the line and immediately started advertising the Mount Lowe excursion in its own pamphlets, magazines, tourist guides and eventually in a neon sign on its headquarters building.

Mount Lowe quickly became a perfect symbol of the healthy, geographically diverse Southland. A 1907 Pacific Electric brochure about the site captured what the trip entailed. In language typical of the promotional campaign, the pamphlet claimed the journey began when the train left the depot at Sixth and Main Streets which, "by the way, is the largest and by far the most elaborate and ornate in the world," for a trip that "is

The view down the Great Incline. The stairs at left were where visitors got off the cars from Rubio Canyon. Originally they led directly to the Echo Mountain House, the grand hotel built by Professor Thaddeus Lowe in 1894 only to burn to the ground in 1900.

Babe Ruth at Wrigley Field. He was a frequent winter visitor to Los Angeles, made several movies here and generally enjoyed the climate. The Babe was out to play in a charity game for L.A. orphans sponsored by the Knights of Columbus in December, 1919 when Yankee manager Miller Huggins tracked him down on the Griffith Park golf course to break the news that Boston had sold him to New York. They signed the papers a few days later at the Rosslyn Hotel. So L.A. played a role in The Curse of the Bambino that kept the Red Sox from ever winning a championship. The baseball gods aren't sadists, of course—they lifted the curse with the passing of the twentieth century.

conceded by all travelers of discriminating taste to be one of the most charming in the world."

Passengers traveled northeast to the loading platform at Rubio Canyon. Here, they exited the standard-gauge Pacific Electric car to board the Great Incline cars, each specially fitted with a very steep pitch to the seats so everyone could see as the car rose thirteen hundred feet on three thousand feet of track at a maximum grade of sixty-two percent. At the top of the Incline, passengers arrived at Echo Mountain and the site of the Lowe Observatory. Most travelers then boarded the narrow-gauge Pacific Electric observation cars for the five-mile trip on the Alpine Division of the Mount Lowe Railway to ascend another fifteen hundred feet up the mountain. On the way, the passengers were treated to eighteen bridges and one hundred twenty-seven curves. The longest piece of straight track measured only two hundred twenty-five feet.

After "this wonderful five miles," the car arrived in front of Ye Alpine Tavern. The Swiss chalet was constructed of local granite and Oregon pine, finished in its natural tone. The centerpiece of the interior of the tavern was the sitting room with its rows of rocking chairs and a huge granite fireplace with the legend inscribed above, "Ye Ornament of a House Is Ye Guest Who Doth Frequent It." Outside were hiking and mule trails to Inspiration Point one-half mile above the tavern or to the top of 6100-foot Mount Lowe.

The second most popular mountain resort in the Southland was Mount Wilson, just east of Mount Lowe. Thaddeus Lowe had originally planned to build his "railroad in the clouds" on Mount Wilson, but it was already controlled by the Mount Wilson Toll Road Company, which had other plans. The owners opened their tariffed pathway in 1889. Initially it was wide enough only for two wagons. Horses and burros were for rent at the bottom, or adventurers could climb on their

Rates at Mt. Lowe Tavern and Cottages

In Effect October 1, 1927.
(Subject to Change Without Notice)

European Plan
American Plan
Weekly and Monthly Rates
Housekeeping Cottages
General Information

Pacific Electric Information Bureau

Phone MEtropolitan 7400

Sixth and Main Streets   Los Angeles, California

SPECIAL TWO-DAY OUTING $7.50 From Los Angeles $7.10 From Pasadena

Round Trip Ticket to Mt. Lowe
Four Delicious Meals and Accommodations Over Night
MT. LOWE TAVERN and Cottages ALL INCLUDED

Inside a 1925 pamphlet about Mount Lowe, you not only got an idea of how the line ran up the mountain, but also the sort of rates you would have to pay once you got there. The illustration is a copy of a mural at the Pacific Electric Building.

Right: The Great Incline was reached by a Pacific Electric special that left from the headquarters building at Sixth and Main. The cars were named Echo and Rubio after the local canyons with a backup called Alpine. The cars went 2,950 feet straight up the hill to Echo Mountain.

Postcard view of the Hotel Rubio. The station for the Great Incline and and hotel were on the upper portion of this oddly shaped structure while the dining room and dance hall were on the lower level. It was destroyed by a flood in 1909.

CABLE INCLINE 3000 F.T. MT. LOWE RY

own or take a carriage. By 1915 cars started using the trail, but it remained a challenge. In his 1915 book about "motor rambles" in California, Thomas Murphy observed that the trip down Mount Wilson "proved as strenuous as the climb, and the occupants of the rear seat were on the verge of hysteria most of the time."

The first of the many Mount Wilson observatories was erected under the auspices of Harvard University in 1889. A small hotel with a veranda overlooking the plain below followed in 1905. There were tents and cabins to go along with the hotel. But Mount Wilson was never as popular as Mount Lowe. The road up to the hotel was a difficult ride or drive, and not the thrilling engineering marvel that Professor Lowe's trolley was. The Mount Wilson hotel itself was much smaller, and considerably more mundane than Ye Alpine Tavern.

Besides these permanent lines, the Pacific Electric was also used to transport large groups to special events. The Air Meet in the Dominguez Hills in 1910, the 1927 downtown parade for

Passing through the Granite Gate at 4,072 feet. Below the gate was the mile-wide, thousand-foot–deep Grand Canyon.

The Alpine Tavern, prior to the remodeling in 1924-1925. Both of these photos were purchased at the Tavern gift shop. c. 1910

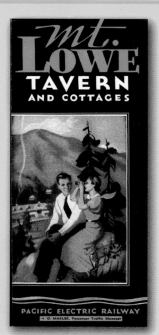

One of the last Mount Lowe pamphlets made. The date the traveler visited what was called inside "The Southland's Ideal Year-Round Mile-High Vacation Resort" was June 24, 1935. Fifteen months later the Tavern burned down.

Right: Pacific Electric spot in *Sunset* magazine advertising several of its chief tourist routes. Mount Lowe is at the top of the list.

Left: Group photo taken on Echo Mountain at the top of the Great Incline. The white building behind is the Mount Lowe Observatory. July 1920

Mt.Wilson
6,000 feet high

Every day in the Year
your own car or by stage

Mount Wilson was named for Benjamin (*Don Benito*) Wilson, another of those early Yankees to settle in the Southland prior to statehood. The small hotel at the top and the several camps along the way took some grit to get to. The Pacific Electric never ran up this mountain.

Mt. Wilson Wagon Road

THE SWITZER-LAND CHAPEL

Switzer-land was named for its 1884 founder, Perry Switzer. His rustic camp was the first of the many mountain resorts to grace the San Gabriel Mountains. It struggled economically for years, finally falling to a forest fire in 1896. It was brought back to glowing life by Lloyd and Bertha Austin after they purchased the camp in 1912. They gave the retreat its evocative name and built Rock Room with its huge fireplace and several small cabins. But the jewel of the camp was the Austins' beloved Christ Chapel. The money to build it was raised in Southland churches. Mission Inn architect Arthur Benton designed the church and local volunteers lugged all the necessary equipment—including stained glass windows and an organ—by mule and strong back to the site. Nondenominational Christ Chapel, dedicated to "The God of the Open Air," opened in June 1924.

Charles Lindbergh and the visit of the *Graf Zeppelin* to Mines Field (later LAX) in 1929 all drew huge throngs. So cars were pressed into service and existing schedules were radically altered to accommodate the crowds. On the rare occasions when something was going on in other parts of California that did not directly involve Los Angeles (such as the San Francisco and San Diego celebrations for the opening of the Panama Canal in 1915), the Chamber issued pamphlets such as *See California Next* inviting tourists to also visit Los Angeles, where all the great sights described in the publication could be seen by way of the Pacific Electric Railway.

The bus would eventually supplant the trolley as the most common collective conveyance

One of the many attractions of the local mountain camps and lodges was visiting snow. It was a tourist attraction in Los Angeles, rather than the daily, winter misery it was in much of the rest of the country. The snow bank on the left is covering the second Mount Wilson Hotel. The first was built in 1905 and burned down in 1913. The second opened in 1915 and was demolished in 1966. The Snow Horizontal Solar Photographic Telescope is in the distance. It was one of six on Mount Wilson. On the right is the successor of the mule teams and wagons that used to bring people up Mount Wilson. The auto-stage was inaugurated in 1912.

to Southern California's major tourist venues. As early as 1924 Tanner Motor Tours buses were leaving from the Alexandria, Biltmore and Rosslyn hotels on the same routes popularized by the Pacific Electric. There was an "Orange Empire" tour and the Tanner version of the "Balloon Route" trip was called "City, Hollywood, Beverly Hills and Beaches." Capitalizing on the flexibility of a bus, there was emphasis on seeing the homes of movie stars and the individual studios. Tanner offered a "Mountain, Movie, Mission" excursion that went where no tracks were laid, taking the visitors directly to Universal Studios and out to Topanga Canyon, down the coast to Santa Monica Canyon and up to the bluffs of Pacific Palisades. The Gray Line offered the same trips for the same prices, leaving from the Clark or Auditorium hotels in downtown L.A.

The light show put on by the setting sun and the Southland below Mount Wilson. This popular postcard was bought at the Mount Wilson Hotel in 1938.

Charles Lindbergh always detested the newspaper-invented nickname "Lucky Lindy." He planned all his flights meticulously. He was an evangelist for air travel. The photo above perfectly captured the messianic aspect of his character.

Right: Lindbergh toured the United States in the *Spirit of St. Louis* after his return from Paris. As with his stop in Los Angeles, he was greeted rabidly wherever he went. But in Lindbergh's mind, he was demonstrating the reliability of air travel as he flew from city to city. September 20, 1927

The Automobile Club of Southern California was another major promoter of Southern California that wound up boosting the area while concentrating on its established mission. The Auto Club was the first organization to post directional, warning and speed-limit signs on the streets of the Southland and it established the first Highway Patrol, men who drove around helping stranded motorists. It also paid for and published the Major Traffic Plan of 1922, which was the first serious effort to improve L.A.'s bottlenecked traffic.

Like the Chamber of Commerce, the Auto Club was not merely content to lure people to Southern California. It wanted to be sure they could move across the landscape in their motorcars. This was a major concern as the population and number of vehicles exploded in the 1920s. The Auto Club investigated car use in all its manifestations. By the end of the decade it found the family car

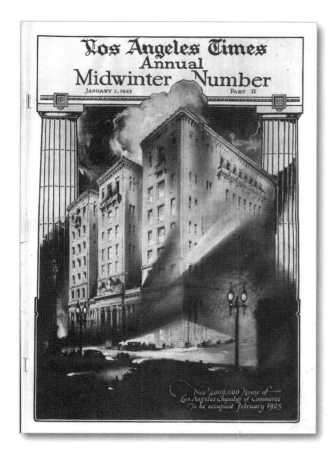

The Balloon Route was the western tour of first the Los Angeles Pacific Railway and later the Pacific Electric. It was named for its shape, rather than any flying apparatus.

Left: One booster giant celebrating another. Featured on the cover of the second part of the *Times'* 1925 Midwinter Number is a rendering of the celebration of the power and influence of the Chamber of Commerce at its very apex—its sixth headquarters on Twelfth Street.

became the most common method for tourists and settlers to come to Los Angeles. There was similar impact in citywide driving patterns. In 1920, ninety percent of workers arrived at their downtown jobs by streetcar; a mere four years later, almost fifty percent were using their own autos.

The Auto Club's sign-posting work had the most obvious impact on the Southland. The first signs went up in 1906 and the effort lasted until 1956 when state and local governments finally took over. Originally, the club took it upon itself to try to make traveling safer and more convenient by putting up signs around towns, something no government entity had done. The labor was provided by the club while the cost of creating the signs was generally split between the ACSC and the local county.

A new opportunity presented itself in 1912 with the opening of the National Old Trails Highway (later Route 66) to Los Angeles. In a perfect example of booster integration, the Chamber of Commerce urged the Auto Club to post the road from Chicago to help lead people to L.A., and the Southern Pacific cooperated by shipping supplies to the sign teams. Local towns contributed funds to be included on the signs, which always listed the distance to Los Angeles. In the first seven years, the club's posting crews had put up more than seven thousand signs. By the time they were done, this strictly local club had placed hundreds of thousands of signs of every possible sort all over Southern California, the western United States, Canada and Mexico.

Los Angeles from an Auto
tells the story of motor-
ing through the South-
land in 1906. Indicative
of the time, it assures its
readers that L.A. is "a
city of destiny, located in
the center of America's
most beautiful and fruit-
ful area, bathed in a
wealth of never-ending
sunshine, her homes
bowered in ever-
blossoming vines, her
business quarter metro-
politan in every sense
and her commerce caus-
ing her to rank among
the great cities of the
western world." A photo
of Frank Wiggins
welomes you to the land
of "The World's Most
Beautiful 'Auto' Ride."

The headquarters of
the Automobile Club,
opened in 1923, was a
suitably magnificent
Spanish Revival Build-
ing at the corner of
Figueroa and Adams.
It is still there in all its
glory, with an original
glass cleaning truck
and many historic Auto
Club-funded road signs.

Auto Club secretaries, like their Chamber counterparts, never knew what the day might bring. Here they are displaying some of the glass collected off the city's streets by the Glass Patrol man leaning against his truck. Broken glass was no joke to drivers in the days before steel-belted tires. Whatever civic boosting the Auto Club did was only a byproduct of its chief concern, which was automobile safety.

The Chamber of Commerce took great pains to promote the popular tourist attractions of Southern
California. But they also worked to publicize the
cultural attractions of the region. One of the first was the
collection of Don Antonio Coronel, scion of one of the
oldest families in Southern California. When he died in
1901, his widow Doña Mariana de Coronel gave his collection of Indian, Mexican and Spanish historic memorabilia to the Chamber for display, not to a museum.

The collection became the centerpiece of the Exhibit Hall. It featured Toltec relics from Mexico, California

Indian artifacts, personal items of Don Antonio and his friends from the Spanish-California period and mementos of Helen Hunt Jackson, author of *Ramona*. On display were Father Junipero Serra's cruets, lamps and books, iron implements made by the Indians of Mission San Fernando and the Mission San Gabriel cattle-branding iron marked "TS" for *Tembolores*, or the Earthquake Mission. In another part of the hall, comple-

menting the Coronel Collection, was the Palmer Collection of Indian antiquities that had been donated to the Chamber by the Southwest Miners Association.

One of the reasons the Coronel and Palmer Collections wound up with the Chamber of Commerce was that there were not many other places to display them in 1901. The Los Angeles Museum of History, Science and Art in Exposition Park did not open until November 6, 1913, and the Southwest Museum (which eventually acquired the Coronel and Palmer Collections) in Highland Park opened a year later. Like so many other things built in that era of constant, startling growth, the Museum of History, Science and Art soon proved too small. The Allied Architects Association of Los Angeles designed a building thirteen times the size of the original, which opened in 1925. This was joined by several other buildings over the years as the Exposition Park cultural area expanded.

But the crown of all the cultural venues in Southern California in the promotional literature was the Huntington Library in San Marino. It was the result of Henry Huntington's urge to collect and his interpretation of Andrew Carnegie's "Gospel of Wealth" which instructed the hyper-wealthy in America to give back to society. So, in 1919, eight years after the Great Merger when he sold his interests in street railways, Huntington endowed a trust creating the Huntington Library, Art Collections and

In 1918 the Hispanic Society of California opened the Casa de Adobe and donated it to the Southwest Museum looming on the hill above. It was patterned after the Rancho Guajome near Mission San Luis Rey, which (along with the Camulos Rancho in Ventura County) inspired Helen Hunt Jackson in her descriptions of Ramona's home. The idea was to demonstrate how life was lived in a Spanish hacienda in the Days of the Dons.

One of the continuing complaints about twenty-first-century Los Angeles is its desperate shortage of park space. One of the major selling points of the boosters was the glory and size of the city's parks, all of which were easily reached by the Red and Yellow Cars.

Left: Eastlake Park's lake on a sunny weekend. The name would be changed to Lincoln Park in 1917 to reflect the name of the local district, Lincoln Heights, and the high school there.

Right: The park of many names. Central Park, Sixth Street Park, and finally Pershing Square. At its crowded apex prior to World War II, one of the attractions was the women's-only section on the west side of the Square. 1938

Botanical Gardens on the grounds of his San Marino estate. Construction of the library building began soon after. Although it would not be completed until 1923, the books started to arrive from New York, and the facility was opened to scholars in September 1920. The entire grounds and galleries were opened several years after Huntington's death in 1927.

Besides promoting places to see great art or trained lions, the promotional literature marked the urban growth of Los Angeles through the early twentieth century. The idea was to present L.A. as a major modern city. To this end, Spring and Broadway streetscapes were commonly used, as were the urban parks—Central (later Pershing Square), Westlake (later MacArthur), Eastlake (later Lincoln), Echo and Hollenbeck. Less common were the more rustic Elysian and Griffith Parks and the distant South

The queen of the city parks was the lavishly landscaped Westlake Park (now the severely truncated MacArthur Park). Lantern slide exhibits using this sort of imagery were shown daily at the Chamber of Commerce Exhibit Room to introduce the Southland and its wonders to visitors.

The lush grounds of the State Normal School on Fifth Street. It was demolished when Los Angeles finally got a branch of the University of California and the main branch of the Los Angeles Library was built on the site.

Park. The Plaza was described in early pamphlets only to disappear as money moved south and then west. It only began to reappear after the opening of Olvera Street in 1930.

In keeping with the promotion of culture and urbanity, boosters typically made a point of the educational possibilities available in Southern California. The local public school system was inevitably lauded as one of the finest in the nation, and was complemented by a series of fine private schools. But by the early 1920s the boosters were fixated on the fact that what they perceived as the most important and dynamic city in the state did not have a branch of the University of California. The Los Angeles State Normal School for the preparation of teachers was inaugurated in what had been Victor Beaudry's orange grove on August 29, 1882, at Fifth and Grand—on what became known as Normal Hill. Fittingly, in keeping with the history of the two cities, L.A.'s Normal School was the second in the state after San Jose's.

Boosters started lobbying for a Los Angeles branch of the University of California early in the twentieth century and were finally successful in 1914. Buildings were constructed on Vermont Avenue where Los Angeles City College is currently located. In what is difficult to interpret as anything but a nose-thumbing gesture from the northern part of the state, the new school did not include the city in its name. Rather, it was termed the University of California, Southern Branch. The athletic teams were included in the slight. In Berkeley, the teams were named after the official state animal, the Golden Bear. In Los Angeles, the teams of the Southern Branch were called the Cubs. When the teams joined the Pacific League in 1926

In its early days at the turn of the century Westlake Park had plenty of room to put in a carriage road to go along with its boat house. This Park photo was sold at the Santa Fe's Fred Harvey House in 1899. Reflecting the triumph of the automobile, the park would be bisected in 1934 when Wilshire Boulevard was extended through it.

Everyday streetcar scenes in the Angel City.

Top left: A LARY car of the D Line heading east along 5th Street in front of the Library, with the base of Bunker Hill behind. Right: A Red Car heading out of the shed next to the Subway Terminal Building on Hill Street between Fourth and Fifth Streets. These cars fed the western district of the Pacific Electric. The Hollywood cars left through the subway that fed onto Glendale Boulevard.

Middle left: The Venice City Hall was served by the Tokio Station. Named for its architectural style, it went all the way back to the Los Angeles Pacific company. Right: At the Los Angeles Railway car barn, cars for Boyle Heights, the Bimini Baths on Vermont, and an "Observation Car Seeing Los Angeles" are being readied for their rounds.

Left: The Pacific Electric did not only carry people around the Southland. This mail car was joined by thousands of freight cars. One of the reasons the Southern Pacific wanted to control the P.E. was due to its competition with the S.P.'s steam freight cars.

In This Issue

MOTORING ACROSS SUMATRA   BEHIND THE BEYOND
By John Edwin Hoag   *By Phil Townsend Hanna*

Initially the all-conquering automobile was welcomed as the great democratizer. It would give the citizenry freedom to go where they chose, when they chose without having to rely on the lumbering streetcars. No machine lasts forever, and these cars are shown in a huge auto junk and parts lot at Fifteenth and Main Streets.

Far left: Looking beautiful but gumming up the streets on the cover of the Automobile Club's Touring Topics.

Left: The California Petroleum/Texaco station on Wilshire Boulevard west of Vermont opened in 1927 and was the boosters' view of how auto culture should look. The station sported bright California tiles, a vaguely Moorish structure and attendants in white puttees. 1928

they became the Bruins, and in 1927 the "Beverly Site" was finally named the "University of California at Los Angeles." (The Berkeley academic establishment did not deign to allow UCLA to award doctorate degrees until 1936.)

No Red Car line was constructed to Westwood to service UCLA. By the late 1920s, the Pacific Electric was no longer building in advance of housing or civic developments. Tracks were also purposely left off Wilshire Boulevard, thanks in great part to Gaylord Wilshire's original vision for his eponymous roadway. It was meant to be a high-class boulevard to the emerging wealthy western end of the city—he deemed trolley cars out of place.

By the late 1920s streetcars were perceived as plebeian eyesores that ruined traffic flow. The "Greatest Interurban System in the World" died a prolonged, sad death, and many of the lines created specifically to connect to new developments were the first to close due to a paucity of riders. After years of steady post-World War II decline, the final streetcar line to Long Beach was axed in 1961. The Big Red Cars were finally killed by the citizenry who demanded personal transportation and became increasingly annoyed with the railroad cars that took up space on their city's terribly crowded streets.

CHAPTER SIX

Most of this scene from *Noah's Ark* is a huge painted backdrop. The mockup of the ark starts at the door. Everything else—from the elephants to the rocks—had to be brought onto a sound stage or outdoor set of enormous dimensions. The ability to put the painter, set director, lighting technicians, actors and animals all together in one place fairly easily was the result of the studios finally deciding to put down roots in Los Angeles. 1928

MOVIE FACTORIES

The first movie studio in Los Angeles was a converted laundry downtown. The first Hollywood studio was a former barn and roadhouse. By the 1930s eight major studios not only dominated the film market, they established huge, intricate factories to produce their product. One of them, Universal, even started its own city.

There had been a fire somewhere in Los Angeles in 1912, so Colonel William Selig sent a crew over to shoot a one-reeler called *Saved By Fire*.

THE BIG BACKDROP

Everyone in Los Angeles lives in a potential movie set. In the days of silent films, the streets of the city were used constantly to shoot chases and comedy bits. The surrounding hills and valleys, mountain streams, lakes and seashore stood in for Europe, the South Seas, the Old West and whatever else was needed. The Chamber of Commerce may have preferred calling Los Angeles "The Land of Eternal Spring," but to Hollywood, it has always been "The Big Backdrop."

MOVIES: A temperamental plant of the specie *genus entertainus*. Native habitat Southern California, but may also be found in sparse growths in Europe and New York. Thrives best under ideal climatic conditions and lives on co-operation.

Harry Brown, "Why Movies Will Stay in Hollywood," *Southern California Business,* 1926

Kathlyn Williams was the first lady of serials. Her *Adventures of Kathlyn* (1913-14) was the perfect Selig feature, since it gave the Colonel a chance to co-star his zoo. It is considered the first of the cliffhanger serials that would remain a Hollywood staple into the 1950s.

One of the most influential aspects of the endlessly variegated promotional campaign ironically was not undertaken to sell the Southland at all. The goal of the film industry was to produce and market another created fantasy—the movies. Yet movie makers portrayed the place where those movies were made in a perfect Chamber of Commerce style. The people were healthy and beautiful. The possibilities of life were limitless. The air was stunningly clear and fresh. Through Sunday rotogravure picture sections in newspapers and movie magazines, everyone knew that the seashore, mountains, deserts and urban scenes they saw constantly on the movie screen all were filmed within a short distance of Los Angeles in a mythical place generically labeled Hollywood.

Before it became home to the greatest dream machine ever created, Hollywood was just another development. Harvey Wilcox bought a one-hundred-twenty-acre tract in the Cahuenga Valley northwest of Los Angeles. Hollywood was incorporated on November 14, 1903 and annexed to Los Angeles seven years later primarily to share the water flowing in from the Owens Valley, since the Cahuenga Valley was agricultural at that time. One of the first advertising pamphlets urged settlers to come "where home life is a sweet song" due to "its altitude—its pure ozone—its perfect drainage—its freedom from dampness and fogs—making Hollywood climatically perfect."

Hollywood would not remain an agricultural district for long. The machines that would change the history of Hollywood and Los Angeles, the movie camera and projector, were patented by the Thomas Edison Company in 1891. In 1908 Edison and his allies formed a trust, The Motion Picture Patents Company, intending to control all aspects of filmmaking and exhibiting in the U.S. The "Edison Trust" and its General Film Company subsidiary were as ruthless as any nineteenth-century robber baron about intimidating and prosecuting those who did not pay licensing fees. In an uncharacteristic oversight, Edison had poor patent protection in Europe. American producers, eager to escape paying the exorbitant fees demanded by the monopolistic Edison Trust, began to use European equipment and tried to elude Trust investigators by finding locations distant from New York and New Jersey to shoot their movies.

The early filmmakers led a very nomadic existence. Chicago, with the Selig and Essanay companies, shared equal billing with New York as the center of the film industry in 1909. The Lubin Company was located in Philadelphia. Selig tried out Jacksonville, Florida, in the winter of 1910. Several films were made in the New Orleans area, others around San Antonio, Texas, and parts of Arizona, but none of these places were suitable for a large film industry. Making movies demanded a place with outstanding climate, varied topography, a large, growing city and space to shoot. Where in all of these great United States could the itinerant filmmakers find such a unique spot?

When part of the flood of Los Angeles promotional pamphlets washed up on the doorsteps of early filmmakers such as William Horsley of Nestor Studios and Fred Balshofer of Universal and Metro Pictures, the industry was introduced to an obscure city across the continent

Several people will be cavorting on an ocean liner when this scene showed up on local movie screens. *Melody Cruise* (1933) is one of the few movies that fit right in with the promotional campaign. It starts off in the frozen east with a ship full of people headed off to the warmth of Southern California. Phil Harris chases Helen Mack all over the state, even through an orange grove, due to his profound ardor.

Tourist photo of a film crew using the St. Catherine Hotel at Avalon as a backdrop. c. 1920

that promised freedom from the recalcitrant weather and uninteresting scenery that plagued America's earliest filmmakers.

Still, movie-making came slowly to the Los Angeles area. Another snap of miserable weather in Chicago caused Colonel William Selig, who had lived in northern California as a young man, to send members of his Selig Polyscope Company to faraway Southern California to try to complete the filming of *The Count of Monte Cristo* at Venice in 1907. The accouterments of filmmaking were very scarce in the far west, and had to be brought along. But the Venice scenes worked out very well. The following year, Selig's director Francis Boggs was dispatched to establish a permanent base in Los Angeles. He rented a vacant Chinese laundry downtown at Eighth and Olive. The first movie filmed entirely in L.A.

came out of the laundry. It was called *The Heart of a Race Tout* and was released on July 27, 1909.

Selig quickly established that not only was Los Angeles much further away than Chicago from the interference of the Edison Trust, but also home to weather that was predictable—in a good way. He sold the property downtown and set up shop at the Mission Studio in Edendale (now part of the Echo Park district) in 1910. *Motion Picture World* called it "the most beautiful producing studio in the world." But it too proved to be too small. In 1914 he opened a new studio on thirty-two acres across from Eastlake Park (and, as noted before, later opened a zoo to go along with his studio).

Before he left for Eastlake Park, Selig had been joined in Edendale by the no-longer-aptly-named New York Motion Picture Company. The Nestor Film Company left New Jersey, in October 1911, establishing a base of operations in an abandoned roadhouse at Sunset and Gower called the Blondeau Tavern, thereby becoming the first film company to settle in Hollywood. Not long after, Biograph, Vitagraph, Essanay and Quality were all filming in the greater Los Angeles area.

Colonel Selig sharing a smoke with a pal from his zoo.

Los Angeles has always stood in for everywhere else. The camera car has California plates. The towed car has New York plates.

Filming *At the End of the World* in Malibu, standing in for the coast of China. Director Penrhyn Stanlaws is standing behind his cameraman, Paul Perry, filming Betty Compson and Milton Sills. 1921

There was never a paucity of locales to pose studio starlets. As the snipe pointed out, "Samson had nothing on Vera Reynolds, pretty little star for DeMille Studio, when it comes to swinging a hammer." She is helping her career at Venice Pier and giving the studio a chance to plug *Almost Human*. 1927

A group from the Morgan Dancers were filming at the First National Studio in Burbank. A stills man hit on the idea of taking them to nearby Toluca Lake to help publicize their movie, *The Masked Woman*. 1927

One of the great filming-cheaply-in-L.A. quotes from early Hollywood is generally attributed to either Samuel Goldwyn or Carl Laemmle. "A tree is a tree, a rock is a rock. Shoot it in Griffith Park." But by the time moviemaking got serious in the Southland the ostrich farm in that park had left, and Chester Conklin, right, had to go to Lincoln Park to film this scene.

By 1918, the film industry was blossoming all over the Los Angeles basin. As early as April 1911, the new industry's chief publication, *Moving Picture World*, published an article called "Los Angeles as a Producing Center." The Chamber of Commerce hyperbole about L.A. having three hundred twenty days of sunshine out of three hundred sixty-five was prominently noted. And the diversity of available locations was another major factor. Twenty miles west of the city were "the pleasure beaches with a score of high-class beach resorts." The amusement piers at various beaches made Atlantic City or Coney Island settings possible. Selig and Biograph were already famous for making marine dramas in the area. Within this same radius were some of the most beautiful homes and gardens in the United States. The San Gabriel and San Fernando missions were nearby. Mount Lowe was a "scenic mountain railway . . . in the shape of a trip from roses to the snow line in forty minutes." By expanding the radius a bit, any manner of western or adventure movie could be made because, "Here is found the necessary rolling country cut up by foothills, treacherous canyons and lofty mountain ranges in the background."

The early motion picture companies are all but absent from the pre-World War I promotional pamphlets. But even if the conservative Chamber of Commerce was leery of movie people, the fans of what soon became the most popular form of mass entertainment in the world knew exactly where their idols worked and lived. The movie industry quickly became the ultimate silent partner in the promotional campaign. A major unwitting player in all this was Carl Laemmle, founder of Universal Studios. He kept getting letters addressed to the anonymous leading players

The beach was always a great place to photograph young actresses. While it may have fit in perfectly with the boosters view of the climatic and healthful delights of the Southland, to the studios it was a way to get their contract players into a bathing suit. Above: Photographer Bert Longworth of Warner Brothers took a trio of dancers from Busby Berkeley's *Colleen* to a perfect rock formation in 1935.

Left: MGM's Mary Doran and Raquel Torres have a tug-of-war for photographer Milton Brown at the Malibu Beach movie colony. 1929

Betty Bronson, Esther Ralston and Norman Trevor present Paramount's exceptional releases of 1926. One of the tragedies of the silent era of Hollywood is how few of the films survived. There was no particular sense of creating anything but disposable entertainment by most of the producers and studio heads. Also, the film stock was nitrate based and as such highly flammable and difficult to store. When talkies came in, silents were so utterly swept away that it took decades before much of an effort was made to preserve early Hollywood. Now both the Library of Congress and the American Film Institute have programs to preserve and restore silents.

Douglas Fairbanks and Mary Pickford, Hollywood king and queen at Pickfair, their castle. They are planting a Douglas Fir tree to celebrate their fifth or wooden anniversary in 1925. The snipe reminded readers that the couple "are ardent promoters of all United States reforestation schemes." Mary Pickford addressed the Chamber of Commerce Board in an effort to get them to support tree-planting as a way to beautify Los Angeles.

Right: Tourist photo of Charlie Chaplin and the photographer's pride and joy.

ers in his movies. Until this time fans were thought to be drawn to movies based on which company made them. But he knew that vaudeville and Broadway were both very much star-driven. So, in 1910 Laemmle lured "The Biograph Girl," Florence Lawrence, away from that studio with the promise of promoting her own name. This was the start of the Hollywood Star System. Mary Pickford, Douglas Fairbanks, Charlie Chaplin, Rudolf Valentino and a host of others followed. Their specific stories differed, of course, but the one thing they all had in common was that these eventual stars all came to Los Angeles.

The worship of Hollywood movie stars—those who could be seen on a large screen in every neighborhood theater in the country simultaneously—led to a star mania that far overshadowed anything generated by the Broadway stage. Soon there were books and magazines devoted to the film stars and their directors. Eventually newspapers would devote endless free space to the new industry: all the studios had to do was supply photographs and access to their players to receive the sort of publicity that had previously been reserved for the baseball industry. Since virtually all of these photos were taken in the vicinity of Los Angeles, the booster campaign got a huge shot in the arm. And the Chamber didn't have to pack up any exhibits for Des Moines.

The position of the film companies in the promotional campaign changed in the 1920s. By the end of the decade, the dust of early filmmaking had largely settled. What shook out was eight

major studios producing hundreds of movies a year, and several smaller ones turning out niche films. Massive investments were made in permanent stages and offices in studio lots covering acres of land. In its 1919 *Annual Report,* the Chamber of Commerce already had noted that work was constantly being done on the studios, so it seemed likely "that the plants of the world's great producers will remain in Los Angeles as permanent institutions." The money that funded the studios was still in New York, but clearly, the creative aspects of the film industry had established in the L.A. area.

By the early 1920s even the once-reticent Chamber of Commerce started including the movie industry in its brochures rather than just mentioning studios in its in-house publications.

When she wasn't playing tug-of-war for photographer Milton Brown at Malibu, Raquel Torres was up at Big Bear frolicking in the snow with Dorothy Janis for Clarence Sinclair Bull's camera. Had the Chamber of Commerce written the caption for the photos they would have noted the two pictures could have been taken on the same day. Since it was a film company taking the photo, the snipe refers to them as "pretty little Metro-Goldwyn-Mayer screen players" seeing if the snow really will "make their cheeks rosy." 1928

Right: Tourist photo of a cabin with artificial snow at United Studios.

Lillian Lucille Ludwig was chosen the "artist's model" of Montana State University due to her "perfect form and rate beauty." Like so many other American beauties, she was drawn to Hollywood. Lillian transferred to the University of California, Southern Branch (soon to be UCLA) and started knocking on studio doors. December 4, 1924

The film industry offered all sorts of employment opportunities to the Southland. Muralist and illustrator Willy Pogany was brought in to create the Egyptian backgrounds for Universal's *The Mummy*. 1932

The snipe written on the back of this photo when "politically correct" wasn't a society-wide concern, refers to Muia and Riano as "African savages brought in from the wilds" for re-shoots on MGM's *Trader Horn*. They are looking at "one of Hollywood's freak restaurants," as the snipe continued. 1929

French journalist Paul Achard wrote *A New Slant on America* in 1931. When trying to explain Hollywood to the folks back home, Achard noted of his visit to Universal City, "Here skiers—there a cannibal hut. A director calls out: 'I must have a desert and twenty camels by tomorrow morning at eight o'clock!' and we know that he will have them. A half-breed child was needed in a half-hour. It was there. Universal built trenches ten miles long for *All Quiet on the Western Front*. Five thousand soldiers were used, with batteries of artillery and all necessary war materiel."

This was particularly true of Universal, which was the only major production company to welcome tourists. Carl Laemmle, who owned the company, played his part in the promotional campaign by widely advertising the opening of his new studio on the old Taylor Ranch near Lankershim Township in March 1915. He brought out special trains full of distributors and theater owners and let movie fans into the new project to see how it all worked. The crowds were so big that Laemmle decided to make it a permanent feature. Bleachers were set up and, for a quarter, people could watch how movies were made. (This ended with the advent of sound pictures that required "quiet on the set." Universal was not reopened to the public until 1964.)

The promoters would have been fools not to take advantage of the free advertising device that studios dropped in their laps. Whenever VIP tourists arrived in Los Angeles they inevitably wanted to get a look at Hollywood and its moviemakers. Whether it was a visiting Congressional committee from Washington or the Prince of Wales, they all booked time at one of the studios

before heading over to Pickfair for dinner with Hollywood's own royal couple, Douglas Fairbanks and Mary Pickford. It all contributed to the aura of the city. Crowned head or common citizen, when you came to Los Angeles you knew it was someplace special. Dyspeptic eastern writers with raging allergies to sunlight and open space could dismiss the place as "Double Dubuque" or "The Seacoast of Iowa," but everyone else wanted to come see where the stars lived.

The Chamber of Commerce refused to integrate the film industry into its promotional literature until after World War I. Although wanderlust and paranoia marked the early years, Southern California had clearly become the center of moviedom by the mid-1920s. But the Motion Picture Trust had been declared illegal, and Chamber

Cecil B. DeMille, Mary Pickford and Sid Grauman, three major players in the booster campaign who promoted the Southland by proxy as they built the film industry.

Top: **Fritz B. Burns** (center, in tie), vice president and sales manager of Dickinson and Gillespie real-estate subdividers, welcomes a film troupe to Palisades del Rey. His company was selling lots on what it referred to as "The Last of the Beaches," since the rest of the shoreline in the L.A. area was already spoken for. 1925

Opposite, top row, left: The Mitchell Studio captured this sister dancing act at their Broadway studio. Most of the early comedy and dancing stars of early Hollywood got their start in vaudeville and the possibility of being discovered for the screen was a draw for vaudevillians working Los Angeles.

Top center: Two L.A. manias in one. Twenty-year-old MGM star Marceline Day in her brand-new Packard. Given the harsh effects caused by the lights and the properties of early film stock and developing chemicals on complexions, like so many silent-era actresses she started at sixteen. 1928

Top right: Raquel Torres managed to carry her acting career from silents to talkies. In one of those only-in-L.A. stories, she was discovered by a director while working as an usherette at Grauman's Chinese Theater. Two years later she was on the screen there, starring in *White Shadows in the South Seas*. The year after that, she was posing in her old uniform for MGM's chief portraitist Clarence Sinclair Bull. 1929

Bottom row, left: The life of a Hollywood player wasn't all great dresses and nights at the Cocoanut Grove. Paramount's Grace Bradley, aka Mrs. William "Hopalong Cassidy" Boyd, smiles gamely for photographer Whitey Schafer in a local ice plant. 1936

Bottom center: L.A. native Betty Blythe was a huge hit playing the *Queen of Sheba* in 1921 and *She* in 1926. The actress visited England that year and performed as a vaudeville headliner. She is seen greeting fans upon her arrival at the Liverpool Railway Station. By 1928 her career was quickly waning. She committed the cardinal Hollywood sin of "maturing" too early.

Bottom right: Louise Carbasse arrived in L.A. from Australia in 1916. Carl Laemmle of Universal saw her screen test and decided to name her Louise Lovely. Her last American film was in 1922 and she returned to Australia. In 2000 the Australian Film Institute named its equivalent of the Oscars "Lovelys" in honor of this first Aussie international star.

Virginia Bruce and Diane Sinclair help MGM to publicize the other big game in town. 1932

Hollywood was on the tourist track before the movie people arrived. A trolley car on the Balloon Route, shown at far right, stopped at Paul de Longpre's home to visit his extensive gardens, above, and see his famous flower paintings.

The big backdrop was not defined by the L.A. city limits. The "old French village" was northeast of town at the oft-filmed Vasquez Rocks.
December 12, 1937

Bottom right: The All Year Club used a contribution from Fox Films to let people know, "Western Movies Are Made Here." It was printed in the 1929 edition of *Southern California Through the Camera.*

members wanted assurance that the movie industry had finally decided to stay in one place before it was brought into the fold as a serious Southern California industry. In a 1926 article, Cecil B. DeMille hammered home the theme that motion picture companies had finally found the perfect home for their productions. He noted that in the last fifteen years the film industry had amassed property worth more than $1.25 billion and that eighty-five percent of all the motion picture production in the world took place in Southern California. DeMille pointed out that to "gain the spotlight of special attention," cities must "have in their midst some peculiar and interesting factor which commands public attention." He was very perceptive about the film industry's place in the promotional campaign. Unfortunately, DeMille was less prescient when he also noted, "I firmly believe that the motion picture will within forty years drive war from the face of the earth."

Less given to flashes of directorial megalomania, producer Joseph Schenck noted in *Southern California Business* that "Los Angeles . . . is the only spot in this country for the really advantageous location of film companies." He put the percentage of movies made in Southern California at ninety, and noted that "the motion picture people have adopted Los

One of the most potent aspects of the promotional campaign was the national knowledge that the stars who so fascinated everyone lived and shopped, as well as worked, in Los Angeles.

Left: Elmer Fryer was sent out to photograph Billie Dove at her Tolucca Lake home, with its all-year garden and swimming pool. March, 1930

Right: The developers of Outpost Estates in the Hollywood Hills aggressively advertised Dolores del Rio's home. It was perfect having the Mexican actress living in one of the Spanish Revival homes. 1928

Bottom left: Postcard folders of stars' homes were the perfect complement for that other staple of Los Angeles tourism, the map of the movie stars' homes. Playing perfectly into the boosters' game plan, the printed notes to the folder starts out, "In a land of perpetual sunshine, many of the Movie Stars have built their homes." Naturally, Mary, Doug and Pickfair grace the cover. 1929

Bottom right: The boosters came to appreciate the positive effect Hollywood had on promoting the city. The back cover of the official La Fiesta program was an ad for the upscale shopping district on Hollywood Boulevard between Vine and La Brea. Quality shops began to abandon downtown Los Angeles during the 1920s and to spread along both Wilshire and Hollywood Boulevards. First-run movie palaces followed. Sid Grauman's first Los Angeles theaters were the Million Dollar and Metropolitan Downtown. He built the Egyptian in 1922 and the Chinese in 1927 on Hollywood Boulevard.

If anything, the coming of sound tied the studios even more closely to the Southland. The initial problems with picking up dialog called for closed sets and constant yells for quiet. The huge trio of boxes in the center of the *Bride of the Regiment* set were to house the noisy cameras. 1929

Right: The coming of talkies proved a boon for local felt manufacturers. MGM's Dorothy Janis is fitted with felt soles for her scenes with Ramon Novarro in *The Pagan*. 1929

The staircase in the lobby of the Pantages Theater on Hollywood Boulevard celebrated two of the key elements of the booster campaign: airplanes and movies.

Angeles—this is their home—and they are proud of the fact." This major effort to assure the city of the industry's dedication may have been spawned by an article in a previous issue criticizing San Francisco for its "unneighborly act" of trying to lure production away. Schenck advised the Chamber readers not to worry about this. Movie production was staying put. "The business of motion picture making has been legitimatized and stabilized and its future is abundantly assured."

As the studios were stabilizing their presence in Los Angeles, they were soon joined by an even newer form of mass entertainment. Radio had just begun to develop in the 1920s, and by 1929 was feeling its way into popular drama, news and comedy shows. As with movies, radio shows were largely produced in New York and Los Angeles. Noting that the manufacture of radios "has become a substantial and successful Los Angeles industry," the Chamber celebrated this development and added that in 1929 there were twenty regularly established radio stations in the Southland.

These stations were praised not only for the infrastructure of plant and equip-

Tourist photo of a group of Shriners watching "talking movies" being made at Universal City. June 5, 1929

Universal City offered 230 acres to film any sort of movie. Director Raoul Walsh's camera is pointed toward the "French" battlefield and away from the autos, corral and general buildings behind him to film a battle scene in *What Price Glory?* 1928

Besides the army of electricians and lighting people, the studios also had to hire teachers for their underage actors. Schoolrooms were set up on the lot and the sets as needed. These fourteen Fox starlets are going to school on their film set at the beach. c. 1932

Film stars often played a personal role in the booster process, none more significantly than Mary Pickford. When she wasn't greeting Congressional leaders or European heads of state at her Pickfair mansion and grounds, she was dedicating highways for the Automobile Club of Southern California, inaugurating routes for local airlines and helping to found and direct United Artists.

In the late 1920s, the main boulevard of Hollywood was a nice mixture of the movie world and the rest of us. In the foreground is the mecca of film-dom, Grauman's Chinese Theatre, with its courtyard of stars' handprints and footprints. Next to it was the Hotel Hollywood, since 1903 the first great hostelry in the city and home to many visiting actors and specialists in the early days. The tall building down the way is the 1927 First National Bank of Los Angeles building. Security First National Bank bought it when First National was wiped out by the Depression.

Advertising booklet for *The Sunshine Special* train route. It started with the Missouri Pacific in St. Louis and joined the Southern Pacific at El Paso. On your arrival, it promised, "Sunny California . . . of the 'pictures'. . . itself a picture- land more colorful and fascinating than any portrayed on the screen." c. 1929

ment they had developed, but for the jobs they provided. Some fifteen hundred "highly-paid Los Angeles artists now derive a large part of their livelihood from the radio," as did more than three hundred technicians. The Chamber knew that events such as football games and the Rose Parade were broadcast all over the nation. Overcome by the booster spirit as always, *Southern California Business* pointed out that as the rest of the country sits "before their base-burners or their steam or hot- water radiators during long sub-zero evenings," those almost-frozen listeners have the opportunity to hear "the sunshine and song and warmth and happiness that come to them over the air from Southern California." Radio announcers inevitably participated in the promotional campaign even if all they did was read the daily weather reports.

Promoters from the railroads to the Automobile Club all attempted to paint the view of Los Angeles as a glamorous, unique place where dreams could come true, but none promoted the place as strongly as Hollywood did, albeit with no concerted effort. The common knowledge that the movies were made in Southern California, and that the stars who so intrigued the country lived there, was invaluable to everyone selling the city of dreams.

The Fox Carthay Circle vied with the Chinese for Hollywood premieres—in this case for *The Good Earth.* There was a large courtyard to set up temporary bleachers and roadway for limousined arrivals. The tower was always illuminated, as was the huge neon sign. The searchlights were brought in for the event. The interior was homage to the westering experience, with murals on the walls and the asbestos curtain. All that remains is the statue of a miner panning gold on the north side of San Vicente Boulevard. Horrifyingly, this magnificent theater was demolished in 1970 and replaced with the most mundane office building imaginable. 1937

CHAPTER SEVEN

The stands and landing area for aeroplanes, balloons and dirigibles at the field set up for the Los Angeles Air Meet in January, 1910. There would be a second meet in 1911.

DOMINGUEZ AIR MEET

It was so typical of the Chamber of Commerce to vigorously pursue the chance to capture the second air meet in history and the first on American soil. It was held in January 1910, a mere four years after the Wright Brothers lifted off from the Kill Devil Hills near Kitty Hawk, North Carolina. As a booster event, it was naturally held in the winter. The meet was the first time virtually all of the two hundred twenty-six thousand people who attended had ever laid eyes on an airplane.

The Grand Central Air Terminal was the Southland's first major airport. Curtiss-Wright operated a flying service and school next to the terminal.

THE GRAND CENTRAL AIR TERMINAL

The Grand Central Air Terminal in Glendale, with its concrete runway, was the Southland's premiere airport at the dawn of passenger travel. When it was dedicated on Washington's birthday in 1919, Los Angeles Mayor George Cryer and fashion maven Peggy Hamilton barely escaped with their lives when they were hit and dragged by the tail section of a tri-motor. The Kinner Motor Company was headquartered here, and the Slate Dirigible was built in a hangar on the property. Maddux Air Lines transferred its operations here from Rogers Field, and Charles Lindbergh piloted the first transcontinental airline service from Southern California to New York from Grand Central. The cramped space of Grand Central led to Union Air Terminal in Burbank becoming the major area airport by the late 1930s, with Mines Field / Los Angeles Municipal / Los Angeles International assuming the mantle after World War II.

There must be a good basis for the fact that California as a state leads in commercial aeronautica; why Los Angeles County has more airplanes in proportion to population than any other county in the United States, and why the metropolitan district of Los Angeles registers more aviators holding United States Department of Commerce licenses than any other city. The basic reason is the same as for the general prosperity of the state, county and city—namely, climatic superiority.

Los Angeles County Spreads Her Wings (Chamber of Commerce, 1928)

Dr. Ford Carpenter is in the rear seat while J.A. Rosenkranz, head of the aeronautical division of the National Automotive and Electrical School, is up front. The duo had been on a twenty-thousand air mile visit to principal American cities to speak on behalf of aviation development.

Ford Carpenter was not a land developer, banker or speculator of any kind. He was one of the least likely major players in the L.A. promotion machine, yet he was by far one of the most influential. A Ph.D. meteorologist from Chicago, Carpenter became the first manager of the Chamber of Commerce's new Department of Meteorology and Aeronautics in 1918. He was every bit as involved in boosting Southern California as Frank Wiggins, but he did so in the careful language and endless lists of a scientist.

After service with the Army Air Corps and the United States Meteorological Service, Carpenter was nationally respected when he signed on with the Chamber to add his scientific voice to the climatic perfection claim. He spoke to numerous groups and wrote articles for dozens of periodicals as diverse as *Aeronautical World, Proceedings of the American Climatological and Clinical Association, Proceedings of the Royal Meteorological Society* and the Automobile Club's *Touring Topics*. Each of the articles was angled to the interests of the individual magazine but the theme remained the same. In Carpenter's often-stated view, Los Angeles was "The Land of the Beckoning Climate."

According to his writings, "the automatic sunshine recorder" at the weather bureau indicated that L.A. had an average of 354 days a year with sunshine, with 172

Snapshot of the Transcontinental Air Transport Ford Tri-Motor at Grand Central Air Terminal. On the back, the photographer noted that the aeroplane was the first transcontinental flyer, and that it was piloted by Charles Lindbergh and christened by Mary Pickford. July 8, 1928

Left: Inauguration of Air Express Service of the long-established American Railway Express Company at Vail Field, Montebello, October 31, 1927. The airport was constructed on land that had been part of the Vail Brothers cattle ranch, while the original hangar was formerly a movie studio. Charles Lindbergh landed the *Spirit of St. Louis* here when he visited L.A. on his national tour following his flight to Paris in 1927.

Manual Arts High School student Jimmie Doolittle was one of the tens of thousands of people who saw his first airplane at the Los Angeles Air Meet. He went on to set numerous speed and distance records, earn one of the first hundred Ph.D.s in aeronautical engineering, be the first pilot to take off, fly and land an airplane using only instruments, win the Bendix and Schneider Trophies for aviation achievement, plan and lead the Doolittle Tokyo raid in 1942, and command the Eighth Army Air Force in England.

cloudless days and only sixteen days with a quarter-inch of rain and five with winds greater than twenty-five miles per hour. Frost was largely relegated to interior valleys and mountains, while fog occurred for more than one hour on only twenty-six days. He argued to a national audience that the Southland's weather conditions were the best in America for flying.

Carpenter had plenty of company when it came to pointing out how conducive the Southland's climate was to aviation. William Garland was not only president of the Los Angeles Realty Board and a major downtown developer, he was also a director of one of the first successful local airlines, Western Air Express. Combining his interests, Garland wrote that "Airplanes will take land values up." He argued that the only national advantage Los Angeles had in 1927 that it hadn't had for a thousand years was its accessibility via modern transportation. With advances in aviation, the far west was now more accessible for both commercial and residential investors. In Garland's view, "By cutting down on the time required to traverse any given route of travel, the airplane has brought a new and highly important factor to the economic structure. But, of even more direct interest to realtors, the airplane's function makes property increasingly more accessible to a greater number of people, thereby tending to increase realty values."

The promoters always sought to portray Los Angeles as the city of the future. So it was

America's
First
Aviation Meet

Los Angeles
Jan.
10 to 20
1910

The pennant which was for sale at the Los Angeles Air Meet made it evident that appropriate pride was taken by the city in the premiere meet in the country where the aeroplane was invented. Still, it was a Frenchman who stole the show. Louis Paulhan was paid $50,000 to bring his aircraft to Los Angeles where he set altitude and distance records. He is seen here adjusting the engine of his Farman biplane for the record-setting long-distance flight.

Bottom right: Florence Stone, actress and wife of meet organizer Dick Ferris, about to be taken aloft by Paulhan. The claim was made at the time that she was the first American woman ever to fly in an aeroplane.

no surprise the emerging field of flight appealed. Therefore, when the Chamber heard there would be an American Air Meet, they set out to capture it. The idea for the meet grew out of the first such exposition in Reims, France, in August 1909. Airmen Charles Willard, Roy Knabenshue and Glenn Curtis contacted Los Angeles businessman and balloon enthusiast Dick Ferris to help raise the necessary money to stage an air meet in Southern California. Ferris turned to the Chamber of Commerce. With the help of the Merchants and Manufactures Association—and the threat of New York state planning a similar meet for the Spring—the Chamber raised over one hundred thousand dollars to provide prize money and build the viewing stands, pathways, hangars and water sources for the thousands of people who were expected to show up for the meet.

The Dominguez Air Meet was held January 10 through 20, 1910, on Joseph and Edward Carson's ranch between Compton and Long Beach. French aviator Louis Paulham, who was guaranteed fifty thousand dollars to compete, established a distance record by flying the seventy-

146

five-mile round trip from Dominguez Field to Santa Anita in one hour, fifty-eight minutes and twenty-seven seconds. He also set a new altitude record at 4,165 feet. Local flier Glenn Curtis bested the favorite Louis Bleriot, fresh from the first flight across the English Channel, in a speed race.

More than two hundred twenty-six thousand people gathered at Dominguez Field to see the flying machines. The air meet was a decided success, netting the promoters twenty thousand dollars and introducing aviation to an ever-growing public. Still, D.A. Hamburger, who was chairman of the Dominguez executive committee as well as a Chamber of Commerce officer and owner of the largest department store in the city, could not help using booster-speak as he rejoiced over the success of the air meet. "The people of Los Angeles should feel proud that it was, and is, the only place in this broad land of ours where in the month of January the atmosphere is balmy, light and warm enough to permit of such a successful meet."

World War I led to dramatic improvements in airplane design, and the 1920s saw an explosion of American interest in aviation. Nowhere was this interest keener than in Southern California. Of the three dozen airports scattered around Los Angeles by the early 1920s, two of the busiest were next to the oil wells that dotted the plain around what is now Wilshire and Fairfax. These adjacent airports, both opened in 1919, had a decided connection with the other new industry in town: their respective owners were Cecil B. DeMille and Syd Chaplin (who was an actor, director and manager for his half-brother Charlie).

This composite photo was a souvenir of the Air Meet. The "airplane" would eventually be moved to a studio on Broadway with the background changed to downtown Los Angeles with the Romanesque City Hall central to the image.

Being involved with an airman in 1910 called for serious hat protection. On the left is Mrs. Louis Paulhan, who accompanied her husband from France; at right is Florence Stone.

Louis Paulhan being carried on the shoulders of admirers on his return from his record-setting cross-country flight. January 18, 1910.

DeMille started Mercury Aviation and tried to establish an air route between L.A. and San Francisco. The planes of the day were not up to the task, however, and the company soon failed. As the film industry took up more of their time, both DeMille and Chaplin sold their fields to Emery Rogers, who combined them as Rogers Wilshire Boulevard Airport. He was killed in a crash in November 1921. His widow sold the fields to land developers in 1923 and moved to a new airport location on Western Avenue and 126th Street, naming it Rogers Field.

Garages and small manufacturing plants all over Los Angeles were turning out airplanes for private use. Otto Timm built the "Pacific Hawk" at the Pacific Airplane and Supply Company in Venice. Nearby, Waldo Waterman designed and built his "Gosling" for the Waterman Manufacturing Company, while Edward Fisk and J.W. Catron were busy designing a triplane. Winfield Kinner developed his "Airster" in his office in the Story Building on Broadway. He eventually moved

The old and the new forms of transportation in SoCal: the oxen-powered Mexican *carreta* in the foreground and what the press always dubbed the "huge" thirty-two-passenger Fokker F-32 airliner. Locally, Western Air Express flew the under-powered behemoths. One of them wound up on Wilshire Boulevard as part of a Mobil Oil gas station called Bob's Air Mail Service. March 4, 1936

By 1939 there were not too many cities in the U.S. that could join a functioning stagecoach and a DC-3 in one photo. This picture was taken to celebrate the inauguration of *The Plainsman,* a new American Airlines cross-country route. May 1, 1939

It was simply not in Cecil B. DeMille's nature to think small. He was convinced he could start one of the world's first airlines and connect L.A. with San Francisco, San Diego and Chicago by air. The illustration is a complete fantasy. In 1919 there were simply no aeroplanes that were of sufficient reliability, power and size to perform the task DeMille had in mind.

his operations to Glendale, where he established a factory and airport that would eventually become the Grand Central Air Terminal.

Like the film business, the aircraft industry slowly shook itself out. The winnowing that began as aircraft became more complex and the government began to invest more heavily in improving their performance, was accelerated by the Depression. Smaller companies began to fall by the wayside. The manufacturers that emerged from the shakeout would build the airplanes that helped the Allies win World War II. Of the companies that began their slow climb to dominance in the Los Angeles area in the 1920s, none was more important than Douglas Aircraft.

Donald W. Douglas left his position as assistant professor of aerodynamics at the Massachusetts Institute of Technology in 1915 to join aviation pioneer Glenn Martin as chief engineer at his factory on South Los Angeles Street. (Martin was a decidedly great groomer of talent—eventually William Boeing, Lawrence Bell and James McDonnell would all spend time with Martin before starting their own companies.) Douglas held the same position for the new Wright-Martin Company when it opened in Cleveland in 1917. Three years later, deciding to strike out on his own, Douglas returned to Southern California. After short stints in two small facilities—including a former film studio off Wilshire Boulevard—Douglas built his own factory at Clover Field in Santa Monica. His first great success was the Douglas World Cruiser for the Army Air Service. Five of these airplanes flew from their home in Santa Monica to Seattle, then took off on the first around-the-world flight in 1924.

The boosters saw several reasons why aviation companies should prosper in Los Angeles. Like all other industries, they had the advantage of working with a unique labor force. In an extensive article published by the Los Angeles *Examiner* on June 13, 1926, and reprinted by the Chamber, Edwin Clapp argued that the climate created "a contented race of workmen. They can make Eastern wages, and live for three-fourths of Eastern costs. The balance they save or spend for the good things in life. The net result is that they are happy, productive and eager to please." These merry laborers were creating the latest aspect of the transportation system. Clapp saw L.A. as being in on the ground floor. "There is going to be a Detroit of the aircraft industry. Why not here in Los Angeles?"

After the wildly successful publicity campaign, Los Angeles became a major aviation center. Granted, the climate was an obvious lure. But the Chamber was very aggressive in using its advertising and business advisory boards to convince early aircraft designers to work in Los Angeles. By the time Franklin D. Roosevelt called for an air force of fifty thousand planes in 1940, most of the smaller companies had gone out of business, but Douglas's airplanes shared Southland airspace with those of North American, Lockheed, Northrop and Hughes. The large companies were supported by numerous specialty companies in the Los Angeles area. Bendix, Aero Corporation, Crawford Airplane Supply Company and Kinner Airplane Motor Company all made aircraft instruments and parts. By 1929 the estimated yearly revenue from producing airplanes and parts in L.A. was twenty million dollars.

A great number of these planes and parts were going into the newly developing airline industry. The bulk of the income of these airlines did not come from selling the few passenger seats

Two key players in the promotional campaign who were doing other jobs. Army Air Service L.T. Lowell Smith on the left, piloted the Douglas World Cruiser *Chicago* on the first round-the-world flight. He is shaking hands with the appropriately-named "Dusty" Rhodes. He is the Automobile Club's field engineer, whose road-charting trips took him to every part of the United States in the earliest days of motoring. 1924

Top left: Donald W. Douglas (left) on an inspection tour of his new Santa Monica plant with Secretary of the Navy Curtis D. Wilbur and Charles Bayer. 1925

The Wings Division for the DC-2 is in the foreground. My father started his forty-two-year career with Douglas riveting these wings. June 11, 1934.

My father took his Kodak Autographic camera to Douglas one day and snapped a DC-2 he helped to build as it received its finishing touches. 1934

available on the early aircraft. Rather, it was all those mailbags in the cargo compartments. The federal Contract Air Mail Act of February 1925 was the start of a viable airline system in the United States. The new law called for transferring of mail delivery from the Army Air Corps to private industry on a competitive bidding basis. This led to the creation of several small airlines all over the country, all of which vied for the lucrative airmail contracts.

Los Angeles had its share of local airlines. One of the first was Western Air Express, incorporated five months after the Air Mail Act. Initially it flew the mail route between Los Angeles and Salt Lake City, carrying only the occasional passenger. But the most interesting of the purely local airlines was Maddux. Its creator was Jack Maddux, a local Lincoln dealer. Full of the optimism so rampant in Southern California at the time, he decided to start his own airline after seeing a demonstration flight of a Ford Tri-Motor. To garner publicity, he hired Charles Lindbergh to plan the first Maddux route to San Diego, which was inaugurated in July 1927. Mary Pickford christened the first flight. San Francisco was added in April 1928. By the year's end, the airline also linked Fresno, Riverside and Bakersfield to Los Angeles. Almost ten thousand people flew with Maddux that first year. In 1929 the airline extended to Phoenix and El Paso and had forty thousand customers.

Charles Lindbergh played a key role in the development of aviation in the United States. He was integral to the inauguration of Los Angeles' earliest airlines and worked with Lockheed on several of the company's designs.

In the photo at left he is congratulating Lockheed designer Jerry Vultee—who would eventually run his own company—on the new, more streamlined and windproof Pyralin cockpit on his Sirius monoplane. February 3, 1930

Below: Western Air Express first flew in 1926 using Vail Field, Montebello.

Maddux's fleet of fifteen Ford Tri-Motors was the largest in the country. In its two years of operation the airline leased space first at Rogers Airport and then Grand Central in Glendale. In November 1929, Maddux merged with Transcontinental Air Transport to form the basis of what would eventually become Trans World Airlines. But in two short years he showed what a local car dealer—or anyone—with some money and vision could build in the wide-open Los Angeles of the late 1920s.

The military also found Los Angeles to be a conducive air environment. The Army Air Corps first flew out of Santa Monica's Clover Field, then Mines Field in Westchester. The U.S. Air Service Reserve was headquartered at Clover Field, while the California Air National Guard flew out of Griffith Park Airport. The weather conditions permitted flying and training all year long with varied geographical situations. The activities at these Army Air Corps bases and the battleship fleet at San Pedro were the only military aspects to be found in the promotional campaign.

GRAF ZEPPELIN LANDS AT MINES FIELD

The Chamber of Commerce never missed an opportunity to take advantage of any aviation event that might come its way. One of the most significant was the chance to host the German dirigible *Graf Zeppelin* on its round-the-world flight. In an effort to demonstrate the reliability of its lighter-than-air, rigid-framed airship for trans-Atlantic commercial service, the Zeppelin company announced a worldwide flight by its *Graf Zeppelin.* The dirigible was only going to land three times once it started its journey, and the Chamber lobbied hard to have L.A. be its Western American stop. It succeeded. The *Graf* landed at Mines Field at dawn on August 26, 1929. That day a half million Angelenos arrived by auto and special Pacific Electric cars to see the massive airship.

The flight had begun at Lakehurst, New Jersey at midnight on August 8, 1929. The *Graf* flew east in its stately fashion, arriving at Friedrichshafen, Germany, two days later. After a stop at Tokyo, it crossed the Pacific Ocean, making landfall on the West Coast of the United States near San Francisco on August 25 and then made its way south, passing over San Simeon to pay respects to William Randolph Hearst (who had helped fund the flight). As the airship neared Los Angeles the next morning, D.W. Tomlinson flew a Maddux Airlines Ford Tri-Motor to guide it to a landing at Mines Field. After showing off the ship, refueling and restocking, the *Graf Zeppelin* took off for Lakehurst, arriving there twenty-one days, seven hours, and twenty-six minutes after it had left Germany. The takeoff from Los Angeles proved to be one of the most dangerous parts of the entire flight. An inversion layer, in which warmer, less-buoyant ground air is kept in place by cooler upper air (and would become a major component in the city's eventual smog problem) had moved in. The layer destroys lift. The heavily-laden airship just barely made it over the power lines that ran along the east side of the field.

Aerial shot of the *Graf Zeppelin* at Mines Field. Those dots in front of it are people and autos. At that time the entire field was east of Sepulveda Boulevard. The street at the top is Aviation Boulevard. August 26, 1929

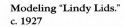
Modeling "Lindy Lids."
c. 1927

The Chamber of Commerce always tried to lure anything involved with the new air industries to Los Angeles. From the 1910 Air Meet to the *Graf Zeppelin* the group had been quite successful. The Chamber also made the winning bid to have the National Aeronautical Association hold its sanctioned 1928 National Air Meet in Los Angeles. Besides all the flying, the Chamber set up an aviation trade fair in conjunction with the exposition. As always, the Pacific Electric cooperated by scheduling special trolley cars to Mines Field in the far western part of the city.

A rare Chamber of Commerce failure involved the proposed new plant of the Goodyear-Zeppelin Company in 1925. The plan was to build a state-of-the-art factory to construct lighter-than-air ships, primarily for the Navy. This was twelve years before the *Hindenburg* disaster largely ended the short-lived era of the dirigible. An exploratory team was sent

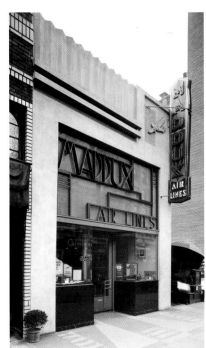

The headquarters for the short-lived Maddux Air Lines was at 510 W. Sixth Street downtown. These interior and exterior shots were taken by Los Angeles photographer J. Howard Mott, one of the first purely architectural photographers in the United States. 1928

Grand Central Air Terminal was the first Southland airport to have concrete runways. Far more typical of the era was this field at 103rd Street and Western Avenue.

One of the six aerial markers pointing the way to Mines Field. This one is on the Firestone Tire and Rubber Company property. Another was on the roof of the Automobile Club Building. The original idea was to guide pilots coming to Mines for the National Air Races on the minimal instruments of the day. Additional directional arrows would eventually point the way to other landing fields. The enormous neon sign on top of the Bendix Building at Twelfth and Maple Streets was originally meant to be a location finder for pilots. 1928

to several cities by Goodyear-Zeppelin to determine the best location for the new factory. The Chamber prepared a prospectus on Los Angeles and shepherded the visitors around the city to peruse prospective sites.

The plan was to build the plant next to an airfield. In Los Angeles, the municipal airport was only leased. As was the case with Rogers Field in 1923, the lease might not be renewed—and then where would Goodyear-Zeppelin be? In the end, Akron, Ohio, already home of Goodyear Tire and Rubber, was chosen. Besides being the leading producer of rubber products in the United States, Akron also owned its municipal airport. The loss led the Chamber to successfully fight to get Los Angeles to purchase Mines Field in 1928, making it the official municipal airport.

Goodyear-Zeppelin may have rejected Los Angeles, but the flourishing movie studios came to play their part in the emerging air industry. Stunt pilots joined their cowboy counterparts in finding ways to make movies more exciting. The best-organized group was the Thirteen Black Cats, led by Frank Clarke. It was formed in 1925 and flew out of Burdett Airport at Western and 102nd. They

The first flight of Maddux Air Lines, from San Diego to Mines Field. It was piloted by Charles Lindbergh and "copiloted" by Will Rogers. Jack Maddux, center, flew up with his family and members of his Board of Directors.

Interior of the Flying Club at Grand Central.

Inauguration of the Pickwick San Diego to Seattle air and bus route. The passengers are boarding the bus for the overnight trip from Grand Central to San Francisco. The overall west coast trip took 23 hours and 10 minutes. June 26, 1929

American Airlines personnel welcome the new Douglas DC-2 to Grand Central. 1934

The Goodyear blimp *Volunteer* over the Curtiss-Wright Flying Service hangar at Mines Field in Westchester. February 7, 1932.

Below right: The blimp was headquartered at the lighter-than-air station at the Goodyear plant at 66th and Central. Eventually a hangar would be built in the southwest corner of the property. 1930.

established set rates for their stunts. Crashing a plane was $1200, changing from a car to an airplane cost $150, as did a parachute jump into the ocean, while a head on collision with a car went for $250. The big-ticket item, at $1500, was to blow a plane up in mid-air while the pilot parachuted out.

By the end of the 1920s, Los Angeles was firmly established as an air center. Besides the flying schools, manufacturers, nascent airlines and special aviation events, the city was chosen as the western terminus of the first hybrid transcontinental air route. This nationally-promoted effort to link the nation by regularly scheduled airplanes combined with trains was the result of an idea developed by Transcontinental Air Transport. Charles Lindbergh was hired to map out the route. The plan was for night travel by rail, while daylight was spent in the air. On July 7, 1929, a Pennsylvania System passenger train pulled out of New York. It traveled through the night to Columbus, Ohio, where a TAT Ford Tri-Motor picked up the passengers, flying through the day to Waynoka, Oklahoma. From there, the Santa Fe train traveled all night to Clovis, New Mexico, where another Tri-Motor carried them to Los Angeles. The whole trip took about forty-eight hours, cutting more than two days off the train-only journey. This transcontinental route was premature. It lost $2,750,000 in eighteen months and was discontinued. It was not until the development of the sleeper version of the Douglas DC-3 in the mid-1930s that transcontinental air flight became economically feasible.

Ford Carpenter was right. Los Angeles was the perfect home for the aircraft industry. Yet

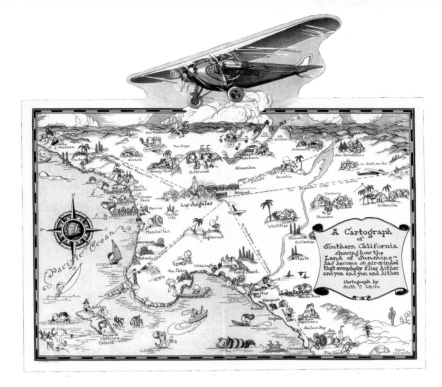

HERE, GENTLEMEN, *is the Ideal Spot in all America for the* Aircraft Industry

The remarkable industrial growth of Los Angeles County may be attributed to:

Natural year 'round climatic advantages

Tremendous population growth

High per capita buying power

Abundance of contented labor

Low building costs

Low cost power

Largest concentrated market on Pacific Coast

Splendid transportation facilities

Economical access to Pacific Coast and export markets

Flying conditions are as nearly ideal the year 'round in Los Angeles County as anywhere in America.

U. S. Weather Bureau reports over the last 50 years show an average wind velocity of 5 miles per hour . . . . 355 days per year with sunshine . . . . 274 days per year when the temperature is neither above 80 nor below 40.

17 manufacturers of airplanes and 9 manufacturers of airplane motors have already located here.

There are 25 or more aviation schools, 2200 aviation students, and more than 3,000 pilots in Southern California.

6 passenger transport companies operate 11 regularly scheduled lines out of Los Angeles, which is the terminal for 4 air-rail and 2 air-mail lines.

These are facts which the manufacturer of aeroplanes, motors or parts can turn to his profit . . . . for these conditions have a tremendous effect on production costs and successful operation . . . . and they are not paralleled elsewhere in America.

Air-Minded LOS ANGELES COUNTY

Complete detailed surveys and information supplied, upon request, by INDUSTRIAL DEPT., LOS ANGELES CHAMBER OF COMMERCE

despite his best efforts, neither Los Angeles nor anywhere else ever became the Detroit of aviation. However, the Southland got more than its fair share. The Chamber's Industrial Bureau had been successful in attracting the aircraft industry. As was the case with automobile drivers, Southern California was home to more aviators than anywhere else in the world. In 1928, of the 5,653 licensed or identified civilian aircraft in the United States, California ranked first with 801 (New York was a distant second with 558). The strength of the aviation industry was one of the reasons Los Angeles was able to weather the Depression better than most American cities. It also put the Southland in a perfect position to play a major role as part of America's World War II Arsenal of Democracy.

Chamber of Commerce ad in *Aviation* magazine that perfectly sums up the uniting of climate with industrial development.

Top left: Western Air Express cartograph of the Southland for the aviation-minded. 1929.

Camera plane for *Wings*, the winner of "Most Outstanding Production" at the first Academy Awards ceremony held on May 17, 1929. Hollywood not only helped advertise the Southland through its movies, it offered work to thousands of laborers, designers, technicians and pilots. 1927

In 1940 the Works Progress Administration built a model of the city of Los Angeles to help with urban planning. The finishing touch is the tallest building in California from 1928 to 1964—the Los Angeles City Hall.

CITY HALL

The Los Angeles City Hall thrusts into the sky, seemingly so modern and traditional at the same time. Gleaming white in the sunshine, taller by half than anything else in the city for its first half-century, it became the immediate symbol of the city for the boosters. And it still is.

The ruins of Long Beach and Compton following the big earthquake on March 10, 1933 became a tourist attraction completely unsanctioned by the booster groups. All through the promotional campaign the most famous threat to the Southland was ignored. After the physical ruination and hundred twenty deaths wrought by the magnitude-6.25 quake, the problem could no longer be ignored. The Chamber of Commerce led in the efforts to design and pass new building codes.

THINGS YOU WOULDN'T SEE
IN THE PROMOTIONAL CAMPAIGN

The boosters always painted the rosiest possible picture of Los Angeles. Writers were not always so sanguine. In *A Truthful Woman in Southern California* (1893), Kate Sanborn pointed out that it does rain "and every year an earthquake may be expected. I have experienced two, and they are not agreeable."

The especial message that the All Year Club wishes to bring home to you is that Southern California has one of the finest all-year-round climates in the world, that its climatic advantages constitute an unusual appeal to the visitor and to the home seeker, and that its influence benefits practically everything that touches on modern living and industrial conditions. . . . Taking all things into consideration, no better climate, day in and day out, can be found in the United States.

All Year Club, *Southern California All the Year,* 1922

The Chamber of Commerce studied practically everything about Los Angeles. One of its studies of tourism found that sixty percent of visitors to the city either stayed outright or returned as settlers, establishing the very direct connection between tourism and population growth. But the Chamber discovered a problem: prior to World War I, practically all tourism occurred during the winter months. Southern California, it seemed, was perceived as Florida west. Mild winters, but those summers must be brutal.

The first Chamber effort directed solely to making tourism a year-round thing, was *Los Angeles as a Summer Resort,* first published in 1902. Much of the text focused on the region's outdoor delights. There were descriptions of the seashore, mountains, camping, fishing and the tent cities at Coronado and Catalina Island. The final section, typical for the era, was on the agriculture of the area.

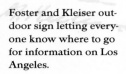

Foster and Kleiser outdoor sign letting everyone know where to go for information on Los Angeles.

But whether the reader wanted to hike or farm, the Chamber promised, "It appears as if nature had selected Southern California to show what she could do at her best, in the shape of a climate that approaches so near to perfection as to leave scarcely a loophole for captious criticism."

The Santa Fe Railroad pitched the same theme in a pamphlet called *The Land of the Afternoon: Summer in Los Angeles, California,* (1907). But this was a railroad publication: the benefits of Arizona, New Mexico and the entire Southwest were mentioned. Los Angeles was featured

Harry Chandler (1864-1944) came to Los Angeles suffering from tuberculosis in 1883. He eventually became son-in-law to Harrison Gray Otis, publisher of the *Los Angeles Times* (1917-1944), land developer supreme and creator of the All Year Club. Chandler and Henry Huntington were the two most influential men in the twentieth-century development of Los Angeles.

since "it would be difficult to imagine a more favorable location . . . midway between the snow-bound Sierra and the sunset sea." Even when it did warm up in L.A., the lack of humidity made a ninety-five-degree day in the Southland more comfortable than an eighty-degree day in the East. The Santa Fe wanted the reader to be assured, "The summer climate of Los Angeles . . . is the most comfortable experienced by any city in the world."

Guides often made the same point. The Hollenbeck Hotel published a booklet called *Vistas in Southern California* in 1893. It quoted essayist George Wharton James' observation that "the glorious combination of winter and summer beauties in immediate proximity appropriately designates the Southland as 'Our Switzerland-Italy.'" *Newman's Directory and Guide of Los Angeles and Vicinity* noted in 1903 that people are simply wrong to "suppose that the climate of July must necessarily be insufferable."

Despite these early efforts, as the 1920s dawned, tourism to Southern California was still overwhelmingly a winter affair. This imbalance led *Los Angeles Times* publisher Harry Chandler to found a new organization dedicated to increasing tourism to the Southland and balancing it throughout the year. He dubbed his idea the All Year Club.

The apocryphal story of how the Club was started has Chandler sitting in his

office listening to a hotel owner bitterly complaining that her establishment was empty during the summer. More likely, the idea germinated after the sharp economic downturn following World War I. The robust agriculture, film and oil industries ensured Los Angeles' prosperity, but tourism was way down. Just as the promotional campaign was reaching full crescendo, the Interstate Commerce Commission estimated the volume of visitors to Southern California had dropped almost forty percent in the first five months of 1921.

Determined to meet the problem head on, Chandler enlisted the Chamber of Commerce, Los Angeles Realty Board, Automobile Club and Merchants and Manufacturers Association to help found the All Year Club. Primary financing for the organization came from the Los Angeles County Board of Supervisors, with additional funds supplied by companies directly involved with the tourist industry. It would go on to become what the *Saturday Evening Post* called "the most efficient come-out-and-see-us-sometime organization in the land." Eventually three hundred sixty similar groups sprang up around the country—all patterned after the All Year Club of Los Angeles.

The first organizational meeting was held on May 1, 1921. Funding—an initial campaign expenditure of fifty thousand dollars—was arranged by the last week of June, and the first ads were in Midwestern and Southern newspapers on July 17. The results were immediate. While tourism for the first half of 1921 had been a disaster, August of that year surpassed the records set in previous years. The campaign proved that well-executed ads could bring people into the re-

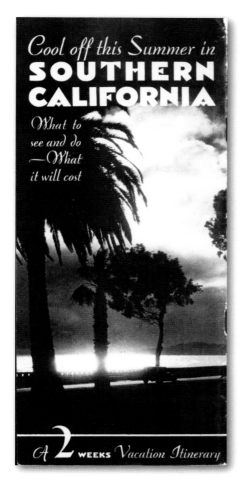

gion despite a poor national economy, and that people would come in the summer months if they believed the weather was fine.

After the success of the first round of ads, the AYC executive committee continued the campaign, focusing on tourism, leaving the expansion of industry and population to the Chamber and other groups. The AYC team also decided to keep the emphasis on attracting summer visitors. They chose a three-fold objective for the newspaper and magazine ads and the pamphlets: "The copy would have to be especially alluring. It would have to reflect Southern California in every phrase and illustration. It would have to compel to action."

The railroads helped fund the AYC and were beneficiaries of the successful tourist campaign. After the second campaign from March to June 1922, railroads reported increases of thirty-five percent to forty percent in ridership, while Southern California hotels reported from fifteen percent to seventy percent occupancy increases, depending on how tourist-oriented they were.

The winter counterpart of the summer pamphlet. It directed the reader how to spend a month in Southern California. This reflected the visiting pattern that was still prevalent in 1931. Winter visitors tended to stay longer.

By the 1920s and 1930s Main Street was home to cheap theaters, where you could see three features for one admission and risque entertainment of all sorts. By this time Main Street had all but disappeared from the promotional campaign. It had become the cut-rate zone of L.A., and that was not the city the boosters wanted to portray. c. 1928

"World Museum," 510 So. Main St. Los Angeles.

Using data obtained by the railroads, the AYC claimed to have brought at least one hundred thousand more people to Southern California in the summer of 1922 than the year before.

The third year of the campaign called for an even larger net to be cast. The East joined the Midwest and South as a target audience. Fifteen national magazines and more than fifty metropolitan newspapers carried the ads. This time the ads were first placed in January, with a full schedule of seven hundred twenty lines of text twice per week for seven weeks for the larger cities and once a week for the smaller ones. The theme was always the same: Los Angeles has the greatest climate in the world and the summers are as invigorating as the winters. The Club began calling Southern California "The Vacation Land Supreme."

The ads were typical of the modern, more graphically-oriented approach adapted by advertisers everywhere in the 1920s. Gone were the simple recitations of facts and endless prose. With the AYC ads, a key illustration dominated the presentation, generally of some bucolic Southern California scene with the text revolving around it. One ad urged readers to "Decide Now to Spend Your Vacation in a Different Place." Another promised "The Children's Greatest Summer,"

Many
VACATIONS IN ONE

Visitors who have been all over the world tell us that Southern California offers a greater variety of attractions, more ways to have a good time—more to see and do and remember — than any other single resort area anywhere.

The map below illustrates the amazing diversity of Southern California's scenery. This map is made from an actual Hollywood motion picture studio "location" chart. Rarely do the movie-makers have to go more than 200 miles to obtain any type of scenery needed for a story laid in a foreign land. You have seen these places on the screen. Now you can make them part of your vacation.

[5]

while another noted that "We 'Film the World' in Pictures Here." The imagery and text changed, but the message never wavered: Grab the next train for L.A.

The two main pamphlets published and distributed by the All Year Club were *Southern California All the Year* and *Year Round Vacation Land Supreme*. Both pamphlets pushed the familiar themes. *All the Year* assured its readers that the summer months offered "balmy rainless days and cool nights." According to the United States Weather Bureau, the average temperature of the last forty-seven Junes was sixty-six degrees Fahrenheit, seventy degrees for July and seventy-one for August. As "a land of infinite variety," the Southland gave the tourist the choice between beaches or snow, allowing the individual "to select your own climate."

Unlike the typical Chamber of Commerce pamphlet, *All the Year* was devoted exclusively to fun in the sun. Women in bathing suits were copiously illustrated, as were golfers, polo players and especially drivers. By 1922 when the AYC published the first edition of *All the Year*, automobiles were increasingly becoming the transportation of choice for locals and tourists alike. In the illustrations, cars drive in splendid isolation through redwood forests in northern California and through "a hint of Asia Minor" along a palm-lined drive in Los Angeles. People happily motor by "a plunging trout stream," "by the surf's edge," and by a desert cactus since "'Sahara' is at the boulevard's end." The AYC assured tourists that "For the motorists there is a virtual infinity of delight in Southern California."

Urban scenes were always featured in the publications. The most common in *All the Year* were Spring Street (known as "The Wall Street of the West") or Broadway cityscapes and eventually the new City Hall. What few industrial scenes made their way into the pamphlets were clean and vast. The industry unique to L.A. was not ignored. As a cameraman shoots a group of actors in

The unique diversity of topography to be found in Southern California was always a key to any organization promoting tourism. The All Year Club promoted outdoor sports more aggressively than the Chamber of Commerce, but both of them made it a key to the L.A. experience.

Left: In its Official Tourist Guide for 1933 the All Year Club tied the benefit of varied scenery in with the movies and why they were filmed locally.

The 150th anniversary of the founding of Los Angeles in 1931 celebrated all things dear to the heart of the boosters. It was only natural that there would be a float honoring the City Hall.

New and the old. The Romanesque County Courthouse across Spring Street from the new streamlined City Hall. 1928

Juanita Burns was an aviatrix based in L.A. Flying her locally produced Timm Collegiate that she dubbed *City of Los Angeles*, Burns claimed to have set an altitude record of over twenty-eight thousand feet on December 28, 1931, but her instruments malfunctioned and she could not prove it. This label was printed in an effort to raise money for her proposed solo flight around the world. But 1932 was the nadir of the Depression; the flight never happened.

Left: A deck of playing cards celebrated both the Days of the Dons and the modern city.

Right: Fokker Tri-Motor in a publicity shot over the new City Hall and Civic Center. 1929

Southern
CALIFORNIA
All the Year

The promoters always aimed at portraying Los Angeles as the most modern of cities. In 1926 the Los Angeles Tennis Club wanted to stress its up-to-date approach and had "Dick" Whittington photograph the ancient and modern approach to the sport. You will notice the modern girl is the one with her chin up, looking superior.

The first *All the Year* pamphlet. There is the barest nod to "Home and Farm and Industry." The aim is at the visitor, and a picture is painted of a city flooded with sunlight, healthy, happy people, plenty of fun things to do, excellent roads for motorcars, mountains to climb, movie-making to watch and lots of beaches where the water is fine. 1922

Spanish costume, the caption reads, "A movie set takes you to Spain, Siberia or the South Seas." The AYC was much quicker than the Chamber to pick up on the obvious interest tourists had in the film business.

Southern California: Year Round Vacation Land Supreme tells a similar story. It claims that the L.A. area is "the All-Year Playground of America." Great pains are taken to explain that the Los Angeles plain is different from the rest of the state due to the unique geography and topography that exists south of the Tehachapi Mountains and west of the Sierra Nevadas. Besides being "the Ideal Home for Every Sport" that exists for the tourists, there is also the chance to see professional baseball played by the Los Angeles Angels and the Hollywood Stars of the Pacific Coast League at Wrigley Field on Avalon Boulevard, noted as being "one of the finest" stadiums in the Pacific Coast League.

A later, often-reprinted pamphlet was called *Southern California Through the Camera*,

While City Hall became the boosters' perfect symbol of the city, the Civic Center of which it was a part never coalesced as the classical governmental center that so many urban planners and City Beautiful proponents had envisioned. From the Broadway side, the County Building and Hall of Records just seem like oddly configured buildings on a chaotic streetscape.

"God Bless America" was one of the songs sung at the dedication ceremonies for City Hall on April 28, 1928. Irving Berlin was in town writing for Hollywood, so he came over and sang his most famous song to inaugurate the new building.

consisting of fifty pages of photographs with captions. The only industry illustrated is movie-making. Several major tourist attractions, such as the Huntington Library and the Hollywood Bowl, are shown. Photos of downtown are featured, with the caption, "Metropolitan Los Angeles—the Lure of a Great City." Along with the typical scenes of horseback riding, golf, tennis, snow- and water-skiing and swimming at the beach, other nearby attractions such as La Jolla and Tijuana ("Mexico's Monte Carlo") are also illustrated. The only writing that accompanies the captions and photos in *Through the Camera* is an essay called "A Story that the Camera Cannot Tell!" The editorial assures its readers that though "Climate cannot be pictured . . . it is an important factor in your vacation, for good health and good spirits are results of good weather." The writer notes that there is an ongoing discussion "as to which is the most luring of the two principal seasons in Southern California." During the winter, "Successive days of rain are rare; nine days out of ten are delightful with warm, brilliant sunshine and cloudless skies. Nights are bracingly cold with infrequent frosts." While mountains may be capped in snow, "A mile below their ice-locked summits oranges ripen in the mellow sunshine." In the summer the air is "dry and keen." But be warned, "There is almost a chilliness to the evening air." So tourists were encouraged to bring a light wrap "but leave your umbrella at home."

The All Year Club had been a success. By the end of the Depression tourist trends had

SOUTHERN CALIFORNIA

.. *through the camera* ..

Southern California Through the Camera was one of the All Year Club's most popular publications. It was oversize and printed in rotogravure like *Pictorial California*, which was partially funded by the Chamber of Commerce. The AYC confined its booster muscle to the Southland, however. *Through the Camera* reminded its 1930 readers, "Only those who have been here know the almost limitless number of ways to have a good time found anywhere are here plus the added attractions of climate and scenic grandeur." *All the Year* featured a similar theme, but was digest size and slightly less profusely illustrated.

reversed. Sixty percent of tourists now visited during the summer. By 1938 tourism was second only to oil and ahead of citrus and movies as the largest individual source of primary income in Los Angeles. In that year, 1,634,834 visitors spent more than $22,224 an hour in the city. New publications such as *The Official Vacation Guide to Southern California* and *Sightseeing Map/Los Angeles City and County* were not as seasonally specific as the earlier All Year Club publications.

The All Year Club and the Chamber of Commerce received plenty of help from the tourists themselves. Visitors took home not only their tales of sunny Southern California, but photos as well. In the late nineteenth century, it was common for local photographers to have mounted pictures of local attractions for sale to the tourist trade. The Blanchard Studio was the major photo purveyor. Its biggest offering was what they called "Mid-Winter Scenes," the kind that inevitably showed some part of the city with a profusion of flowers surrounding it.

Postcards took over from photographer's views as the twentieth century dawned. Five years after postcards were introduced at Chicago's Columbian Exposition in 1893, the federal government gave private printers permission to sell postcards. They were cheaper, more readily available, easier to mail and usually more fanciful. Los Angeles-themed cards often poked fun at the lousy weather in the East, extolled the virtues of a healthful city, or depicted oranges on trees, in boxes or whimsically.

Simply talking to neighbors about their California adventures was not enough for some visitors. Several published their own memoirs. Mina Deane Halsey called her book *A Tenderfoot in Southern California.* It is a comic story of her 1908 adventures in Los Angeles, on Mount Lowe and Catalina and at Arrowhead Hot Springs. Others visitors became "natives" quickly and

HONEYMOONING

MEMORABLE honeymoons. The "trip of a life time" on life's most auspicious occasion. A never to be forgotten journey that will make conversation through the years. New places to go each day. The lure of ocean, mountains, orange blossoms and palm trees.

32

IN ROMANCE LAND

ROMANCE in the land of the Dons. The flavor of old Spain. Memories of the days of *el capitan*, when dashing *caballeros* once played and sang, and beautiful senoritas looked shyly down through latticed windows... Romance land.

31

The All Year Club was much more likely to use fun-in-the-sun images than the other booster groups. They also featured romantic images when called for. 1930

Above left: Another wrinkle in the ever popular oranges-and-snow motif. Inside, there is a photo of the "young lady, a guest of the Arrowhead Springs Hotel, [who] picked oranges on the hotel grounds twenty minutes before she was photographed with the snowman on the front cover." While it was published in Los Angeles, *Pictorial California* was a rotogravure magazine designed to advertise the attractions of the entire Golden State. When it started in 1926, the Los Angeles Chamber of Commerce was one of the major contributors and helped in its distribution while its photo service, Keystone, oversaw publication. Readers were urged to subscribe to the monthly magazine "for your friends back home." It cost three dollars per year "to any address in the world." The tone is the same as the other promotional publications, except that it takes a statewide view.

The Tropical Ice Garden in Westwood Village, proving once again that absolutely anything was possible in L.A. The tent covering is to keep the sun off the ice. 1939

trumpeted the benefits of their new home. Playwright William C. DeMille remembered the first time his brother Cecil B. returned to New York from Hollywood in the spring of 1914 for the premiere of *Squaw Man*. William noted, "My brother had become a complete Californian in six months, and now regarded New York with amused tolerance and all its inhabitants as weak, ineffective slaves of a dying civilization."

Cecil wanted William to come out west and help him write the scenarios for his movies. William was initially reluctant to leave New York, but

Los Angeles, as befits a tourist town, had many moderately priced hotels aimed at the traveler. The premier hotel of the city kept changing. In the nineteenth century the stagecoach race from the harbor to the Bella Union and Pico House was always popular. The Van Nuys at 4th and Main played host to William McKinley and Teddy Roosevelt. William Howard Taft and Woodrow Wilson stayed at the Alexandria at Fifth and Spring, as did Charlie Chaplin and most of the other original Hollywood moguls. By the 1920s there was a constant competition between the Ambassador on Wilshire (where Lindbergh spoke) and the Biltmore on Olive at Fifth (where Einstein spoke).

on his eventual arrival in L.A. found his brother had not been exaggerating. Even this dedicated New Yorker could not help but admit, "The state was living up to its reputation; delicious warm sunlight; a soft, semitropical breeze; the dry desert smell in the air. It was perfect." He couldn't help himself. Like the people from Iowa and Missouri he met who had gone to Los Angeles to die but had been "wooed back to life by the omnipotent climate," he became an avid Californian.

Even the tourists who did not stay to swell the ever-burgeoning population helped the local economy. The Chamber joined the AYC in celebrating tourism's rise to the second-largest industry in Los Angeles. Francis Shanley, the president of the Southern California Hotel Men's Association, noted that by 1926, L.A. and vicinity had two hundred fifty million dollars invested in guest rooms for visitors. The general prosperity of the country had given people the means to travel, and the promotional campaign led them to Southern California. Shanley wanted everyone to know that tourists would find a city that both welcomed them and was prepared for their arrival. Besides the many first-class and tourist hotels, there were tourist camps outside the city and many apartments that catered to short-duration guests. Visitors from all social strata would find a city with an

The Ambassador Hotel opened in the wilds of western Los Angeles on January 1, 1921. To the west were the Pico oil fields. To the east were Westlake Park and Downtown. But around the hotel was pure luxury. The Cocoanut Grove opened April 21, 1921 on the Wilshire side and rapidly became one of the premier nightspots of the Hollywood crowd. The Gaylord, one of the classiest apartment houses in the city, opened across the street the same year.

By the early 1920s, the All Year Club and Chamber of Commerce were as equally rabid in promoting automobiles over streetcars as the Auto Club. They were perceived as the wave of the future and promoted at every opportunity. Still, in 1927 the Cajon Pass took some nerve to tackle. Note that the signs are courtesy of the Auto Club. The Old Trails Road was on the way out as a highway designation. It was becoming Route 66.

expanding commercial base.

While not experiencing the same phenomenal percentage of growth as Los Angeles, the whole country was urbanizing to an unprecedented degree. The 1920s marked the first time more Americans lived in cities than in rural areas. Every modern advertising method was used to make sure that Los Angeles got more than its share of the urbanizing trend. To help in the campaign, the Chamber hired its own photographers for the first time. They worked directly for the publicity department, which supplied photos to anyone who would make use of them. The first was Arch Dunning, who was hired away from the excellent *Daily News* photography staff in 1923. When he put away his camera to move up in the Chamber's Publicity Department in 1928, his place was taken by freelancer Newton Berlin.

The Chamber also utilized photo agencies. The first, Keystone, was the largest in Southern California. In 1926, the Chamber went one better by hiring former Wide World photographer Eyre Powell to create a photo service funded by the Chamber and the County of Los Angeles, operating out of the Chamber's headquarters. The Powell Service proved to be a real boon for the Chamber. In 1928, it was estimated that it received two million dollars worth of publicity for the twenty-five-thousand-dollar contract with Powell. Also initially funded by the Chamber and County was the oversized photo magazine called *Pictorial California* that featured the beauties of the Golden State with a minimum of text.

By the 1920s every one of the booster organizations was firing on all cylinders. The All Year Club had increased tourism, the Chamber of Commerce

Two earmarks of the L.A. experience. Mediums were indicative of what historian Robert Glass Cleland referred to as Angelenos' propensity "to support new movements and worship strange gods." Or, as *Times* columnist Lee Shippey observed, "Not all the residents of the City of Angels are sure of heaven, but there are very few who haven't bought some kind of ticket to it." Spiritualists like Valli, above left, were staples in Hollywood movies and novels based in L.A., but *never* seen in the promotional campaign. Equally celebrated, even revered, in the campaign was the Southern California real-estate developer. The two promoters shown here are envisioning Vermont Avenue Knolls in South Los Angeles. January, 1928.

Lots of ink was spilled claiming L.A. had the biggest this and most impressive that. Well, it also had the smallest store in the country, as reported by International News Photos. It is the Jaffe Candy Store on West Seventh Street, with a thirty-seven-inch frontage. June 24, 1930

brought in new industry and watched the population grow daily, Sunkist started using romantic labels on their citrus fruit crates, and the Automobile Club worked to improve traffic and touring in Southern California and had already posted sixty-eight thousand signs on thirty thousand miles of road. Whatever did not fit in the rosy picture the boosters were painting was ignored.

Chief among these local problems was earthquakes. In 1906 the Chamber of Commerce published a pamphlet following the San Francisco earthquake that noted Los Angeles is five hundred miles south of that northern city, a distance "equal to that of Charleston, South Carolina to Washington, D.C." It claimed that the kind of destruction visited on San Francisco was impossible in Los Angeles because "Geologists say that the rock formation underlying the city of Los Angeles is of such a nature that it is as safe from the danger of earthquake as any locality in the United States."

The All Year Club was the booster organization most willing to display people cavorting at the beach in bathing suits. But none of the promoters ever used overt sexuality to sell Southern California. Main Street was a hotbed of theaters devoted to the talents of the ecdysiast. These glum looking women were dancers at the Follies Theater and had been booked on charges of "indecent exposure and lewd-acting." The photo appeared in the *Examiner*'s news pages, not the "Mid-Winter Edition." 1939

Right: Tourist photo of the aftermath of the Long Beach earthquake. 1933

Moving companies did huge business in Los Angeles throughout the 1920s. According to the census reports, in that decade the population of Los Angeles increased by 761,475. With the promotional campaign largely put on hold due to the Depression, the population still increased 266,229 from 1930 to 1940.

The boosters would cling to their official view until the Long Beach-Compton quake of 1933 showed it to be clearly ludicrous. But the tactic of noting how far Los Angeles was from some danger was a common booster tactic. In an 1889 pamphlet, the Chamber noted that L.A. was more than eight hundred miles from the Apache uprisings and in 1942, the All Year Club reminded everyone that Chicago was closer to Berlin than Los Angeles was to Tokyo.

The very real problems of Southern California so neatly sidestepped by the boosters were investigated in increasing depth during the 1920s. During that decade, the most common author of jeremiads about the city was Louis Adamic. He was an immigrant to the U.S. from Slovakia, a veteran of World War I and a working-class curmudgeon of the first order. He argued that Los Angeles "is a young city, crude, wildly ambitious, growing." Much as novelist Nathanael West would be a decade later, Adamic was fascinated with the midwesterners who came to Los Angeles. He saw them as "retired farmers and crossroad grocers and small-town dry-goods and hardware merchants who have worked like slaves and swindled like hell all their lives, made their little stakes, sold out, and come to California to rest, regain their health and 'enjoy' climate and scenery, to live in bungalow courts and eat in cafeterias."

"Sam the Watermelon Man" in City Terrace. The booster campaign was aimed at Anglo Americans or northern Europeans of some means. A working-class district like City Terrace would not have appeared in the campaign, and black people never did. The spirit of "Jim Crow" was alive and thriving in Los Angeles throughout the promotional era. Mexicans, Chinese and, to a lesser extent, Japanese periodically were portrayed in photos, but only in their national costumes to stress their otherness and picturesqueness. African Americans had no such costume and so were not illustrated, even in this stereotyped, demeaning way.

The Mighty Porciúncula periodically turned on the city and went berserk. In this case sweeping away the Seventh Street Bridge. Nature was always illustrated as benign, earthly beauty. Never a danger. 1905

The Industrial Bureau of the Chamber always stressed "Clean Industry." The Ganahl Lumber Yard workers—one of whom was black—would never have been used by the promoters.

Right: Wayward youth and crime of any sort was not denied by the promoters, just ignored. The girl being escorted by her lawyer, was one of three Hollywood High School students who testified against one Don Courtney on a contributing-to-the-delinquency-of-a-minor charge. She "told of shaking dice with Courtney, the stakes to be her honor against $1000."

Two other aspects of urban life ignored in the campaign were crime and politics. All of the boosters—especially the Chamber of Commerce—worked tirelessly to support or defeat candidates and ballot measures. But unless the measure directly affected them, they tried to stay behind the scenes. One of the downsides to the city's auto culture was bank robbery. Hard to do if you have to jump on a bus or streetcar to make your getaway. Early armored cars that delivered money to banks were formidable things.

Right: The base of Olive Hill at Hollywood and Vermont was often home to elaborate political signs. In this case, novelist and Democratic nominee for governor Upton Sinclair's campaign to End Poverty In California. 1934

Below: Job Harriman, campaigning openly as a Socialist, was very nearly elected mayor of Los Angeles in 1911. The Southland has a long history of being willing to listen to any political belief. The Communist Party USA was very active in the area, and published its suggestions for a local election in 1931.

Working Class
AGAINST
Capitalist Class
Election Platform of the Communist Party of U. S. A. L. A. Section

WORKERS OF LOS ANGELES!

Vote for the candidates endorsed by the Communist Party

SAM SHULEM
for Councilman, District No. 9

EDWARD SANDLER
for Member of Board of Education

These candidates have pledged to carry on a struggle for the following demands of the workers:

1. Immediate unemployment relief for the Workers' Social Insurance Bill!
2. 7 hour day and a substantial increase in wages!
3. Repeal of the anti-working class Criminal Syndicalist law!
4. Immediate release of the Imperial Valley Prisoners!
5. Full economic, political and social equality for the Negro masses!
6. Against the legal lynching and for the immediate release of the 9 young Negro workers of Scottsboro, Alabama!
7. Free speech and free assemblage for workers in Los Angeles!

The city these "small-town" transfers built was little more than "a huge, exaggerated village; an Iowa or Kansas small town suddenly multiplied by five hundred and some of its Main Street buildings grown twelve stories high." Adamic saw them as pawns in the grandiose schemes of the "super-Babbitts" of the Chamber of Commerce who were determined to make "this great region of eternal spring" into "the *biggest* city in the world." As Adamic saw it, "Possessed by a mad and powerful drive . . . they are grim, rather inhuman, individuals with a terrifying singleness of intention; they see a tremendous opportunity to enrich themselves beyond anything they could have hoped for fifteen or twenty years ago. . . . They have their fingers in every important economic pie in the region. They work hard, harder than any other group of people in town."

Adamic was just the most prolific and volatile of the many writers and social critics who had sport with Los Angeles. The articles that were so full of wonder at the turn of the century at the growth of the small, far western city, were more commonly looking on with some bemusement by the 1920s. Writing in *Harper's*, Sarah Comstock shared Adamic's astonishment with the number of "go-getters" and "long-legged bumpkins" in the city, "a strange street

Mexicans were rarely mentioned in the promotional campaign. Generally it was the Spanish past of the Days of the Dons that was celebrated. The costumed Union members at left fit in with the ambiance desired by the boosters but their banner puts them out of bounds. The Chamber of Commerce and Merchants and Manufacturers were adamantine, frantic even, in their opposition to unions.

rabble, yokels rubbing elbows with cheap sophistication," all engaged in a "feverish circle in which everybody is selling something to everybody else." To her, Los Angeles was a "giant infant of a city," but purely American. "Power-madness, speed madness, the selling mania, which may be summed up in general as our Fourth-of-July complex—our insane American lust for hurry, noise and glare—are here seen in the *nth* degree."

Life, a humor magazine that predated by a decade the news magazine of the same name, had a special issue poking fun at the booster mentality called its "Cal!forn!a Number." The cover featured a huge sun labeled, "Native Sun! Copyright registered California Patent Office Sacramento," shining down on an "outing of the Iowa Society." The magazine is filled with jokes, poems, cartoons and illustrations poking fun at the state in general and Los Angeles in particular. The latter is noted as "the only large city in the United States whose population manages to subsist wholly on air. The climate supplies part and realtors supply the rest."

Among the observations on the inhabitants of the Golden State is a "sermon" from Stuart Little:

> Consider the Californian! From sunup to sundown and even after he beateth the cymbals
> and shouteth in a loud voice from the housetops that he is a native son. He disturbeth

Life's "Cal!forn!a Number" had lots of fun with the boosters. Typically, even if things were labeled California and if jokes were being made, they were aimed at Los Angeles. February 26, 1925

Nevada far into the night as he crieth that his is the wonder state, and he harasseth the tourists with tales of its wonders. . . . He painteth the future of California in fiery letters and pitieth the inhabitants of other states, and in so doing he sometimes stretcheth the truth.

The demonstrable success of the Los Angeles booster campaign in the 1920s transformed the city. The Chamber of Commerce proved as able in luring industry as it was in growing the population. So successful and omnipresent was the campaign that it led to national magazines lampooning the city. But just as the Chamber had made itself at home in its block-wide, eight-story headquarters on Twelfth Street, and while the census takers were finding out that the population had grown 114.7% during the 1920s to 1,238,048, making it the fifth-largest American city, the stock market was unraveling.

This economic collapse of the 1930s caught the boosters by surprise. Ever since 1924 they had been gearing up for the 1932 Olympics. It was an event they were sure would carry the name of Los Angeles "again and again into countries where it will do this city good—a dollar-and-cents good." Just as the wildest dreams of the most ardent boosters were coming true, a worldwide depression descended ever more darkly over "the Land of Eternal Spring."

CHAPTER NINE

The "Pageant of Jewels" motion picture electrical parade at the 150th anniversary of the founding of the city took place on September 11, the eighth day of the ten-day celebration. All of the major studios had floats; this is producer Samuel Goldwyn's contribution. 1931

150TH ANNIVERSARY AND 1932 OLYMPICS

A sesquicentennial celebration in 1931 and the Olympics of 1932 represented the culmination of all the promotional efforts and the greatest international advertisement possible. And yet, they also represented the last gasp in a long half-century of dedicated effort in a promotional campaign that suddenly ended. How bittersweet it must have seemed to those who had worked with Frank Wiggins.

In this Douglas Aircraft photo, two Rosie the Riveters—the one on top with a rivet gun, the other with a bucking bar—are working a on fuselage. They are following the clothing suggestions laid out in Douglas' 1943 Hints to Women Aircraft Workers which noted, "Dress For The Job. Don't let glamour interfere with your work. You can wear working clothes and still be attractive. Time is wasted in dolling up like a movie star." 1944

WORLD WAR II IN LOS ANGELES

BOB ther than offering up 21,761 of its sons to the military services and its freshly minted movie stars to Liberty Bond drives, Los Angeles played only a minute, largely agricultural role in the World War I. Twenty-three years later, Los Angeles was second only to Detroit in war-related industry. The city was a leader in aircraft manufacturing, shipbuilding, oil production and popular entertainment as well as a major port of embarkation for the Pacific Theater of Operations. The Chamber of Commerce's Industrial Bureau had done its job well.

Ever since he had retired from his business in Los Angeles and gone to Long Beach to live . . . he had felt like a has-been. There was a new generation in the Chamber of Commerce, where he had once been a vice-president. They called him an old-fashioned booster. They said his stuff was corny.

Timothy Turner, *The Man Who Got Lost in the Fog*, 1941

Mrs. Elizabeth Hicks Gross, La Fiesta queen and granddaughter of the first La Fiesta queen in 1894, Mrs. Emeline Childs. She is being crowned by leading booster and businessman William May Garland, dressed up as an archbishop. It is indicative of how common Catholic iconography was to the campaign due to the reverence for the Franciscans and the Days of the Dons myths. 1931

A s befits a book of short stories about Los Angeles, Timothy Turner's *Turn Off the Sunshine* (1942), is full of crazed failures, dropouts and rejects from the movie business, immigrants on the economic fringe of society and old people mesmerized by the inevitable passage of time. One from the latter group is the retired businessman, William Russell. On a foggy evening, on his way to get the streetcar to Long Beach, he stops at a Main Street bar. He is a man out of his time. A true booster, even a former officer with the Chamber of Commerce, the sort of man who praises the L.A. fog for keeping the heat down, not the kind that "goes through you like a . . . knife" as San Francisco fog will do. He is a slightly foolish figure, drinking too much, before finally getting on the streetcar. He was a booster whose boosting days were over.

A decade before, William Russell may have been a figure of some derision to writers such as Louis Adamic, who poked endless fun at the booster campaign, but he certainly would not have been portrayed as an archaic has-been. The Los Angeles promotional campaign that had been at its ultimate frenzied, hyperbole-spewing height during the Roaring Twenties, barely had time to celebrate Los Angeles doubling its size before the Dirty Thirties closed in. As it became increasingly evident that the Great Depression was not going to be a mere bump in the economic road, the Los Angeles promotional campaign gradually sputtered out.

At first the Chamber tried to keep a stiff upper lip in the face of the horrible economic news. Chamber president John C. Austin urged everyone to think positive thoughts, arguing that if people acted and believed that the Depression was going away, it would. Former President Calvin

Spanish dancers were brought out to celebrate the 1930 opening of the Sepulveda Tunnel easing the passage between West Los Angeles and the San Fernando Valley. Members of the Sepulveda family and the San Fernando High School band were also there. The pass was eventually paved and opened as a state highway in 1935, presenting an alternative to the Cahuenga Pass.

Below, right: The Los Angeles Library system thought that some Depression-ensnared patrons would be reluctant to enter a formal library. So they set up a traveling library for use of the scores of people who spent their days in Pershing Square. 1936

Coolidge's admonition to the Chamber to "continue to build," delivered at the annual meeting on February 24, 1930, was enthusiastically received by the membership and printed in at least two of its publications. But three months into the downturn, *Southern California Business,* the Chamber's magazine, printed a notice on the cover of its January 1930 issue that starting "with this issue, this magazine becomes a general business review of the Pacific Southwest." Gone was any trace of the ballyhoo that had been the hallmark of everything the Chamber did.

Local and national economic depressions had always put a crimp in the booster campaign. The bust after the late 1870s boom, in league with a national depression, had killed the first Chamber of Commerce in L.A. and the statewide California Immigrant Union. The slow economy of the 1890s had

Sara White Isaman published *Tourist Tales of California*, which was printed by Times-Mirror in 1907. It is a series of tales written in a "hick" dialect wherein Aunt Pheba Harrison tells her niece of all the amazing things she encountered along with Uncle Hiram as they journeyed from their Nebraska farm to Southern California.

L.A. contributed many things to the war effort, including Margit Fellegi's "Swoon Suit" for Cole of California. The two-piece suit is rubber-based and completely adjustable due to lacing on the trunks and tie-straps on the bra. The most popular color was "parachute white." 1942

left the new Chamber wondering how best to sell its product. The recession after World War I had led to such worry over the slow tourist trade that the All Year Club was formed. But it took the Great Depression of the 1930s to finally stop the promotion. Beyond the length and gravity of the Depression, the booster campaign had already done its work: by the 1930s, everyone knew about Los Angeles and its many physical and economic attractions.

In a turn that must have sent Frank Wiggins' ashes spinning in his urn, notices appeared in Chamber and All Year Club publications urging tourists to come and enjoy the Southland but not to think of staying. In a reversal of everything previously held dear, the 1931 note went on to say:

WARNING! While attractions for tourists are unlimited, please advise anyone seeking employment not to come to Southern California, as natural attractions have already drawn so many capable, experienced people that the present demand is more than satisfied.

The notice remained on the 1941 edition of the Club's *How to Plan Your Trip to Southern California* despite the improvement in the U.S. job market as the decade turned.

The idea that the demand for new population could ever be "more than satisfied" flew in the face of everything the Chamber of Commerce and its allies had been screaming about for sixty years. But, confronted with a seemingly intractable depression, they saw no option but to cool their promotional jets. As the Thirties wore on, it became obvious that Southern California would not be hit as hard as other sections of the country. After an initial slump, the movie business was back in gear by 1932. Radio only grew stronger throughout the pre-war years. The aircraft and

"Hoovervilles" or "Hoover Towns" cropped up all over the United States during the Great Depression. Herbert Hoover had a sterling reputation, based on his management of efforts to feed a starving Europe after World War I. But the perception that he was doing little to end the Depression or help alleviate the suffering of the jobless muddied his name and caused it to be associated with homeless camps. Over seven hundred men, women and children were living at this one at Alameda and 85th Street. March 12, 1932.

automobile industries remained fairly strong, and Los Angeles continued to be the leading agricultural county in the United States. But the leaders of the campaign no longer felt the city would be able to provide jobs for hordes of newcomers. So they put the megaphones on the shelf.

Two Depression-era events reinvigorated the Chamber's atrophying booster muscle. They were the 150th anniversary of the founding of Los Angeles on September 4, 1931 and the 1932 Olympic Games. The Chamber had been instrumental in the planning and securing of both events that so perfectly fit their intention to celebrate and advertise Southern California. The work begun during the heady days of the Roaring Twenties, when the future of Los Angeles and the United States seemed unlimited and unfettered, was paying off in a radically different environment.

The fiesta surrounding the Los Angeles sesquicentennial turned out to be a celebration of everything the promotional campaign held dear. There was respect for the romantic Days of the Dons, recognition of the major role the harbor played in the life of the city, use of the new outdoor venues—

In 1935 Roy Stryker gathered some of the finest documentary photographers in America under the banner of the Farm Security Administration. Their job from 1935 to 1942 was to help illustrate the impact of the Depression on the small farmer. Dorothea Lange took many of her photographs in California, and was dispatched to Los Angeles' Sonoratown to shoot the homes of Mexican-American farm workers.

The Chamber of Commerce, as official hosts of the Games, produced a pamphlet that introduced both the Olympic venues and the city they were in. Fittingly, the last two pages are a chart on Los Angeles County's climate and a picture of an orange grove and snow-covered mountains.

OLYMPIC GAMES

July 30 to Aug. 14 1932

LOS ANGELES COUNTY
CALIFORNIA

My mother's Olympics ticket. Catherine Albrecht had finished seventh grade at St. Ignatius when the games came to L.A. She took a LARY car with her mother, Mary Conner Albrecht, to the Coliseum from their home in Highland Park.

Below: As expected, Olvera Street's performers were integral to the sesquicentennial celebration of Los Angeles' founding. They might have danced on the first night's "Grand Historical Parade: California Under Four Flags" or the eighth day's "Spanish Barbecue" at Griffith Park.

Xth OLYMPIAD
LOS ANGELES 1932
TRACK & FIELD
OLYMPIC STADIUM
AUG. 5
2:30 P. M.
GEN. ADMISSION
$2.00 31598
A5

The Department of Water and Power also participated in the "Pageant of Jewels" at the Coliseum.

Below: The Olympic torch burning at the Coliseum's peristyle end during the 1932 Olympics. It would be re-ignited fifty-two years later, making the L.A. Coliseum the only place on earth to host two modern Olympics games.

Besides adding another layer of seats to the Coliseum, the Olympics brought on this grass sculpture in front of the peristyle end.

Right: All the local publications were thrilled with the Olympics coming to town. *Saturday Night* covered the arts and assorted topics dealing with the Southland from 1920-1939. *Touring Topics*, below, was the Automobile Club publication edited by the brilliant Phil Townsend Hanna. He had a wonderful eye for talent, and starting in 1926 published photographs by Edward Weston, Ansel Adams, J. Howard Mott, along with the landscapes of George Hurrell, as well as literature, travel and informational articles about Southern California.

the Coliseum and Hollywood Bowl—and a celebration of the recently-developed industries that put Los Angeles in the forefront of American cities. All of this was, of course, surrounded by the sweet fragrance of locally grown flowers. The boosters may have chafed at the slowing down of the ballyhoo, but they could take pride in a ten-day extravaganza that celebrated their vision of Los Angeles.

Nine and one-half months later, the culmination of twelve years of work and planning would commence at the newly-expanded Coliseum. The Chamber of Commerce knew there was nothing like the Olympics to promote a city. Los Angeles chased the event to demonstrate that it was a world-class city and the capital of healthy outdoor living. When the quest began at the 1920 Games in Antwerp, it was evident that L.A. had no hope of hosting the games without a major sports venue. It was the long-held belief of Exposition Park's chief planner, W.M. Bowen, that a major sports stadium should be built in what had been a gravel pit adjacent to the Museum of History, Science and Art. He hired architect John Parkinson to develop plans while booster and developer William Garland tried to bring the Olympics to Los Angeles. Garland brought in the Chamber of Commerce, which convinced city, county and state officials to fund the building of the Los Angeles

The Memorial Coliseum was often referred to as Olympic Stadium during the 1930s. It was always far more than that. Part of the reason for its construction was to help lure the Olympics to L.A., but from its very beginnings, the Coliseum hosted the widest variety of outdoor attractions imaginable, including many of the events associated with the ten-day celebration of the city's sesquicentennial. In the photo below a new layer of seats is being added to bring the capacity up from 76,000 to 101,000. 1930

Come to Los Angeles This Summer for the
OLYMPIC GAMES
(July 30—Aug. 14)

Forty nations will be competing for world honors in 137 events. Never before has this international spectacle been staged as it will be here. Not for at least forty years will the games be held again in America.

Besides, you'll want to see this section whose growth the past decade startled the world. Then there's the cool Pacific Ocean, Hollywood, the old Spanish missions, old Mexico—even a glacier if you want it. And costs, for both transportation and accommodations while here, are lower than ever.

A warm welcome and a cool, interesting vacation await you. Be sure to come.

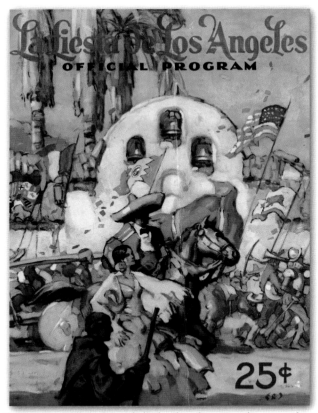

La Fiesta de Los Angeles
OFFICIAL PROGRAM

25¢

Chamber of Commerce handout inviting the country to the Olympics. The other side had a chart bragging that not only was Los Angeles now the fourth-largest city in the U.S., it was more populous than the other four big cities on the coast—Seattle, Portland, San Francisco and San Diego—combined.

Right: The contents of the official program are an amazing mixture of information about the ten-day event and boosterism for Los Angeles. The majority of the ads found a way to incorporate the history of the Southland with their message. The first ad concerns the threat of the area's dropping water level with the imperative, "We must build the Colorado River aqueduct NOW!"

Memorial Coliseum for football, track and whatever else might come up. Excavation began at the gravel pit on December 5, 1921. Fifteen months later, Los Angeles had its Coliseum.

Like Wrigley Field, the Memorial Coliseum was dedicated to honor America's World War I veterans. Unlike its baseball counterpart, it was built with expansion in mind. Originally designed by Parkinson to seat seventy-six thousand, after the Olympics were granted to Los Angeles, the Coliseum quickly gained a new top tier of seats, upping its capacity to 101,000 fans.

The Tenth Olympic Games were held in Los Angeles from

July 30 to August 14, 1932. The international contest occurred during the absolute depths of the worldwide Depression, which caused real fear that the classic might be canceled. But no one can throw a party like L.A. The Chamber of Commerce was the official host of the Games and went to work to organize the city and get it ready for the great event. For the first time, an Olympic Village was built for the athletes—on vacant land in the Baldwin Hills. A swimming stadium was constructed next to the Coliseum, and the Olympic Auditorium on Grand Avenue was built as the boxing venue.

The Chamber played a major role in creating the La Fiesta celebration, in securing the Tenth Olympiad for Los Angeles and in promoting both of them. But these were only specific events. The population of the city continued to grow, but the Chamber was no longer interested in pulling out all the stops to spread the message of the perfect life to be found in Southern California.

My father, Pius Alphonsus Zimmerman was an example of the new immigrant to Los Angeles. He was born on a farm near Richardton, North Dakota, in 1908. His parents were German immigrants and he did not learn English until he went to that great Americanizer of the early twentieth century, the public school. Pius became one of the great American archetypes—a farm boy in the Midwest reading of the great mechanical advances of the twentieth century by the light of a coal-oil lamp. His initial impressions of aviation and its possibilities came from magazines. He became completely hooked when a barnstormer flew into Richardton in 1924, selling flights in his World War I surplus Jenny. Pius kept his ticket from that short flight the rest of his life.

He may have become hooked on aviation, but as the oldest boy on a farm, Pius was not able to go to school beyond the eighth grade and had an endless number of immediate, earth-bound chores to deal with. It took five years after his first flight to convince his father, Franz, to let him go to East St. Louis to attend Parks Air College. Two years later, he returned to the farm and provided the technical expertise as his half of an investment in an American Eagle biplane. While flying above Dakota highways he often noted cars going faster than he was in the teeth of

When the 150th birthday celebration came along in 1931, City Hall was only three years old and was just beginning its life as the ultimate symbol of Los Angeles. It is only fitting that it was celebrated along with the harbor, population growth, Hollywood and aviation as examples of what the boosters perceived as their greatest accomplishments. The romanticized Spanish past is also part of everything that was celebrated at the event.

Like everyone new to Los Angeles, my father wanted to see where the movies were made, so Fred Larvee took him to Fox Studios on his Indian Chief motorcycle. 1933

That's my father leaning on the fender. He went to Yosemite with some friends. Four years removed from a North Dakota farm, and Dad has plainly gone Hollywood. As World War II was winding down, my father was wondering about his future with Douglas. He reasoned that if the company was going to stay in existence it would always have to test new designs. Besides, that would be the most interesting place for a production guy to be. Next thing he knew he was back in L.A. in the Air Test Division and spending lots of time at Murock (later Edwards) Air Force base, helping test new airplanes and hanging out at Pancho Barnes' Happy Bottom Flying Club. One of his proudest jobs at Douglas was being crew chief on the X-3. Bill Bridgeman may have been the fellow flying the thing, but my father made sure it worked right.

If he needed any reminder of why he moved to L.A., he got a big one his first trip back to North Dakota in 1939.

a prairie headwind. Still, fifty years after the fact he would speak with wonder and amazement about the first time he got the Eagle high enough to actually fly through a cloud.

Pius' uncle, Marcus Zimmerman, wanted to retire to Southern California. He had a whole collection of Chamber publications and had settled on moving to the German colony at Anaheim. He became an investor in an orange grove, and Pius agreed to drive him and his wife out here. Leaving North Dakota in the fall of 1932, following a blizzard, the trio arrived in L.A. three days later and found a city basking in beach weather. Pius delivered his uncle to Anaheim, tuned up the Ford after its arduous trip, helped harvest the oranges and then headed to Santa Monica. Fred Larvee, an old North Dakota friend, introduced Pius to the lead man of the wing division at Douglas Aircraft, who hired him on the spot. He stayed with Douglas for the next forty-four years, loving airplanes and the lack of snow and bugs in his new home. There was one change.

My father kept a "Motor Log" on his trip from Richardton, North Dakota to Anaheim, driving a new Chevrolet Master Six from October 19 to 22, 1933. After battling rain storms through North Dakota and Montana, the Zimmerman crew finally arrived in California. They descended the mountains to San Bernardino. At 11:37 on October 22, dad noted, "Leaving San Bernardino. We are feasting on California oranges. The country from San Bernardino through Riverside, Corona and Anaheim was much too beautiful and interesting to think of keeping a log."

Left: War comes to Hollywood. Universal starlets Evelyn Ankers and Vivian Austin are "shopping" by means of a horse-drawn cab to the admiring eyes of soldiers, sailors and Marines. As the song said, "You Can't Say No To A Soldier," so they hopped on while the civilian walks and smokes. 1944

However well a name like Pius Alphonsus sounded in the small German community he came from, it was a bit much for the land of the palm tree. In L.A., everyone always called him "Zim."

So even without the Chamber's campaign, the pattern remained the same—the population of Los Angeles continued to grow. During the decade when people were being urged not to "come here looking for a job," the population increased by more than twenty-one percent to one and one-half million. People like Zim continued to come for work in the still-burgeoning local industries, and to retire. Visitors continued to stream in at the invitation of the All Year Club. The largest boom in the city's history of booms occurred after World War II, again with no boost from the booster groups. Even without all the groups lustily selling the place, Willis Owen was still right when he predicted in a series of 1924 articles in the Los Angeles *Evening Express,* there was no "knocking the peak off" the growth of the Southland. It would last until "the Pacific Ocean goes dry . . . the climate ceases to function . . . when Henry ceases to build flivvers."

One of the things the promotional campaign did was prepare the city to play a major role in World War II. Only Detroit surpassed Los Angeles as an industrial producer during the war. Henry Kaiser not only built a steel plant in Rialto, he also established a shipyard on Terminal Island. A total of 469 "Victory Ships" were built at Kaiser's Calship, second only to his yard in Richmond, California. Still, in the Southland's war effort, shipbuilding came in a distant second to the aircraft industry. There were six aircraft workers for every shipbuilder, with Douglas, North American and Lockheed leading the way.

San Pedro was one of the major ports of embarkation for the Pacific Theater of Operations. Hundreds of thousands of servicemen passed through the Southland on their way to the island-hopping campaign of the South Pacific and remembered it. When their service was done,

All Year Club ad paid for by the Los Angeles County Board of Supervisors.

There was an acute housing shortage in Los Angeles following the war. Another boom was happening as the city tried to find a way to domicile all the workers who had flocked in for war work and brought their families, Japanese Americans returning from the relocation camps, and hordes of veterans who had seen where they wanted to live as they were moving off to war. One solution was the Roger Young Village. It was a huge camp of Quonset huts set up in Griffith Park on the former site of the National Guard Airfield for homeless vets and their families, and lasted from 1946 to 1954. 1946

they returned by the tens of thousands. The boom of the Fifties was the result of millions of men having passed through paradise as a portal to war.

World War II also let everyone in the city know there is inevitably a price to pay for success. The racial and ethnic animosities that simmer just below the surface of any American city flamed to life in Los Angeles in 1943. The Zoot Suit Riot, during which Mexican-American civilians were beaten by police and off-duty military men, was the worst ethnic confrontation in Los Angeles since the Chinese lynchings of the 1870s. African American people flooded into Los Angeles to take advantage of employment possibilities offered by the war industries. Largely confined to the South Central district, African Americans ran into the housing discrimination practiced by every American city in the 1940s. Many moved into Little Tokyo; housing was available there because the Japanese-Americans had been sent off to federal relocation camps. For the duration of the war, Little Tokyo was known as Bronzeville.

The increase in population and industry exacerbated chronic problems. Water was com-

The brother, widow and children of Captain Cassin Young pose at the San Pedro launching of the destroyer named in his honor. September 12, 1943.

Right: Victory House in Pershing Square was a constant source of activity for visiting military personnel and civilians. It often featured Hollywood stars signing autographs to those that bought war bonds. On the 4th of July, 1942, a "Miss Victory" contest is under way while a locally produced B-25 honoring the Tokyo raid of Manual Arts High School graduate, Jimmy Doolittle is displayed in the south east corner of the Square.

Sixty-one percent of the M-5 light tank was made by Los Angeles area subcontractors. The finished product was displayed at General Motors' Southern California Division headquarters.

Right: The belle of California Shipbuilding Corporation on Terminal Island. Calship built 467 Liberty and Victory ships during World War II, and was second only to the Richmond Shipyards in the Bay Area.

There were lots of reasons to visit L.A. during the war, but this sergeant hit the jackpot. He happily poses between Barbara Stanwyck and Claudette Colbert at a Hollywood event "for the boys."

Right: "Rosie" admiring the cannon shell fired by the B-25 behind her at the North American plant at Mines Field/Los Angeles Municipal Airport. 1943

ing in from the Colorado River to meet new demands. (By the 1960s, water would not only come from the mighty Porciúncula, the Owens Valley and Boulder Dam, but also from Northern California by way of aqueducts.) The fabled air that lured the first group of patients to Los Angeles to find relief from tuberculosis became horribly fouled—the worst air in the country. Smog (smoke plus fog, a term originally coined in Pittsburgh) became the accepted name for the wretched phenomenon that stung eyes and lungs, and precluded children from playing in the sunshine.

The initial outbreak occurred on September 8, 1943, Black Thursday. It was not the first day of air pollution, but it was the worst. By the afternoon, there was an actual daytime dim out. Initially, the problem was blamed on a chemical plant just east of downtown which was man-

ufacturing the butadiene necessary for rubber production. The plant was cleaned up, but the smog remained.

It soon became apparent that smog was much more complicated than one dirty factory. The air was no longer the invigorating source of health that lured Frank Wiggins and so many others to L.A. People with lung problems were counseled to leave Los Angeles and its toxic air. On top of this, a major component in the air problems was the automobile, the wave of the future whose bas-relief is on the grave of the Pacific Electric. This disgusting change to the air of paradise horrifed Angelenos. The climate remained, but the mountains that ringed the city to the north and east were becoming invisible. The L.A. smog was soon grist for the mill of newspapers and magazines around the country that published numerous articles on the decline of the most-promoted city in America.

Hazy air was nothing new in Los Angeles. Juan Rodriguez Cabrillo referred to what was later christened San Pedro as "the Valley of Smokes" in 1542 In 1921, Thomas Murphy, in *On Sunset Highways* lamented the difficulty in finding a clear day to drive to the top of Mount Wilson for the view and finally gave up and went anyway. But this post-war smog was a whole new animal. Miserable and unhealthy. The very antithesis of everything the boosters claimed the city had to offer. Paradise lost. National magazines had a field day. I grew up in Westchester barely three miles from the Pacific Ocean, and we spent many recesses indoors with our heads on our desks because it was too unhealthy to go outside and run around. This was just devastating to the city's view of itself. The photo is looking west on Temple Street in 1957.

A 1957 souvenir of Los Angeles, packed for Los Angeles Smog Corporation. You were guaranteed, "This is the smog used by famous Hollywood Stars!" and assured "No pollutants or irritants removed!"

All of the elements responsible for the promotional campaign changed in the post-war years. The Chamber of Commerce, the largest organization of its kind in the United States, had reached its apex in power and influence during the 1920s. After the war, as the city grew ever larger and more complex, the Chamber lost its power. It became like every other Chamber of Commerce in the country, an organization desperately trying to promote and protect local business interests. In 1956 the Chamber sold its thirty-year-old skyscraper headquarters and moved to a one-story building west of the Harbor Freeway. The Chamber also published a small history called *No Small Plans,* which expressed some embarrassment about the promotional campaign.

The other boosters also retired their megaphones. The Automobile Club quit placing road signs all over the western United States. It became an insurance company, albeit one that advocates better roads, offers help with travel plans and aids members stranded on the highways.

The All Year Club merged into the Los Angeles Visitors Bureau in 1964, no longer eager to lure the nation to L.A. and thereby improve the population numbers and industrial base. Tourism is a major component of the Southland's economy, and the Bureau does what it can to

The Mission Inn in Riverside is a miracle. It has emerged in the twenty-first century every bit as spectacular and eccentric as it was in the early twentieth century. Founder Frank Miller was a leading booster, and the Inn was on every tourist itinerary published by every promotional group. It is the closest you can get to the spirit of the booster campaign.

welcome visitors, much like every other Visitors Bureau in America.

Otis Chandler became publisher of the *Los Angeles Times* in 1960 and turned it into one of the five major dailies in the United States, a world-class paper with Pulitzers to prove it. Long gone were the Mid-Winter editions and General Otis's promotional editorials. It outlived all the independent publications and Hearst papers that played their own roles in the promotional campaign. Sadly, Otis Chandler stepped down as publisher in 1980 and retired altogether in 1997. The final nail in the coffin was the sale of the *Times* to the *Chicago Tribune* publishing empire in March of 2000. Long a part of the promotional engine of Southern California, the Times-Mirror Corporation was no more.

The Goodyear Tire and Rubber Company, the first major eastern factory lured to the Southland, was deemed too archaic to upgrade and closed in 1981. In a fitting L.A. end, just before it was demolished in 1987 the old factory was used as a crash site for the helicopter star of the movie *Blue Thunder*. The Goodyear blimp operations moved south to Carson, east of the 405 freeway, on landfill near the site of the 1910 Air Meet.

The headquarters and plant of Samson, the original L.A. tire company, have fared better. Built to look like an Assyrian palace in 1929, it was just too bizarre to be torn down. After years of molding away next to the Santa Ana Freeway, it was finally turned into a huge outlet shopping mall. The walls not only remain, they have been painted and highlighted in a way they never were before America became a post-industrial country.

Santa Catalina Island continues to be a wonderful getaway for harried Angelenos. The casino building is completely refurbished and sometimes will still feature the big bands that made it famous. The *S.S. Catalina* ("The Great White Steamship") was retired from service and replaced by a fleet of quick and serviceable ferry ships that don't have an ounce of romance to them (and definitely don't have a lower boat deck to go visit with your father to see the flying fish jumping out of the Pacific Ocean). After carrying more than twenty million passengers in its fifty-one years at sea, in 1977, the *Catalina* began to slowly sink into her mooring in the Port of Ensenada, Mexico.

The two coastal sister ships, *Harvard* and *Yale* , did not last out the 1930s. The *Harvard* fetched up on the rocks off Point Arguello in the early hours of May 30, 1931. This put a damper on the already-lessening emphasis on coastal steaming. The *Yale* was retired in July of 1936 and mothballed near Antioch, in San Francisco Bay. During World War II she was revamped to serve as a troop transport for the Aleutian campaign. Once the war ended, the last of the Collegiate Coastal Twins was sent to the ship breakers.

The late, lamented Mount Lowe Railroad and Ye Alpine Tavern are no more. The slow demise of the mountain retreat is a story of changing middle-class tastes and of the unpredictable weather that can visit the normally placid Southland. Echo Mountain House fell to fire in 1904 and Rubio Canyon House was flooded out in 1914. The Depression had been hard on Mount Lowe. The number of visitors declined, and it seemed that people with money were less interested in going to the mountains to walk the trials and relax. Horrendous storms ruined much of the track in 1931 and Ye Alpine Tavern was totally destroyed by fire in 1935. In 1938, Pacific Electric

Possibly the biggest mistake in the history of Los Angeles: condemning the citizenry to their cars. Pacific Electric cars in Terminal Island on their way to their doom at the National Metal and Steel Corporation, where Navy ships and autos had been dismanted before the Red Cars were condemned. March, 1956

petitioned the government to abandon the track. Most of it was torn up. Except for a few foundations of destroyed buildings, a few plaques put up by a Mount Lowe historical group, and the still-visible Granite Gate, little marks the existence of "the Greatest Mountain Adventure in America."

The Pacific Electric and LARY interurban systems have also bit the cosmic dust. The last line, running to Long Beach, was closed in 1963. Their demise condemned all the major public venues built with them in mind—particularly the Coliseum and Hollywood Bowl—to parking nightmares, since the overwhelming majority of visitors must drive cars and park somewhere. Both systems had been on the ropes since at least the 1930s as people clung ever more tenaciously to their automobiles. Conspiracy theorists love to blame the demise of the interurbans on an unholy alliance between General Motors, big oil and the tire companies. This trio clearly shed few corporate tears at the funeral, but there was no saving the Pacific Electric. The reality is that the citizenry killed the Big Red Cars.

All the crazy animal farms advertised by the Pacific Electric are gone, but the long-neglected Los Angeles Zoo at Griffith Park has become a world-class facility. Little kids are not encouraged to sit on the alligators, however, and there is a definite paucity of ostrich races. But in one of those wonderful if rare examples of a nod to the history of the city, a zoo director managed to track down several of the concrete animals that decorated the entrance of the Selig Zoo. They have been

Smiling in the face of disaster at a hardware store in Echo Park on Sunset Boulevard. 1976

refurbished and will eventually be worked into the entrance to the metropolitan zoo.

For all the promotional boasts about having space for millions of people in the basin, now that they are here, it is clear that the local environment can only be manipulated so far. The harbor continues to dominate the West Coast, and Terminal Island grows ever larger with landfill, but there are major problems with water pollution in both the harbor and on the Southland's beaches. Air pollution has been lowered due to fifty years of tenaciously fighting it, but the city still vies with Houston for the dubious honor of having the worst air in the United States. The beloved auto, the symbol of L.A.'s freedom, is a major cause of its air problems and has multiplied to such an extent that driving is an agonizing chore and necessity rather than any kind of pleasure. True, once Los Angeles was a car-obsessed culture. Now Angelenos are sentenced to spending hours a week behind the wheel; so the vehicle may as well have a nice interior.

The whole tangled mess of twenty-first century Los Angeles brings to mind the ancient warning to beware what you wish for. Or in the words of singer-songwriter Don Henley, "You call someplace paradise; kiss it goodbye." To read the eighty- and ninety-year-old promotional pamphlets is to marvel at their rapturous optimism and the certitude of mission. The language is often comically verbose, and the racial and ethnic sentiments are never inclusive, but the Chamber of Commerce and the other boosters desperately wanted Los Angeles to be a world-class city, and for good and ill, it is. The sorrow is that two of the cornerstones of the promotional campaign are key causes in the tragedy of the air of Los Angeles. Automobiles were the wave of the future and the promise of individual freedom. Heavy industry would make L.A. into a serious city

It is still possible to take the iconic Southland photograph of orange groves, palm trees and snow-covered mountains, but you have to work to find it. This is in the northeast section of Redlands, which is making a major effort to retain what few orange groves it still has to honor its traditions, create green space, reduce air pollution and to keep the place livable. 2004

in a way agriculture or entertainment never could. Twenty-five years after all the heady promise of the 1920s, these two guarantors of a brilliant future, combined with the very nature of the gentle breezes, inversion layer and a modicum of rain to destroyed the freshest fresh air that Americans ever breathed.

True enough, "lungers" would not be sent to L.A. anymore, and half the time the natural beauty of the mountains that surround the city isn't visible. Santa Monica Bay might sometimes be a danger to a swimmer's health, housing costs are in the stratosphere and the congested freeways threaten sanity.

But still, the sun is usually out, the days warm, the nights cool. To this Angeleno, staring at the television in stupefied amazement as capricious nature goes berserk in some other part of the country, the pleasure of the still-soothing, welcoming climate of Los Angeles makes any of the other problems bearable. And there's one recurring thought, a thought at least as old as those of Frank Wiggins as he regained his health in the city he would happily promote the rest of his life, "Why would anyone live anywhere else?"

Poor Frank Wiggins. He was key to the growth of Los Angeles and now he is scarcely remembered. The *S.S. Frank Wiggins* was launched by Calship on August 21, 1943. After faithful wartime service, she was sold to a Greek line and eventually sent to the Shanghai shipbreakers in 1967. The Frank Wiggins Trade School was started in 1925, only to have its name changed to Trade Technical Junior College in 1954. The A. Phimister Proctor bust of Frank—paid for by twenty thousand one-dollar donations—that once graced the vestibule of the Chamber of Commerce's headquarters on Twelfth Street, did not fit either the space or attitude of the much smaller Bixel Street headquarters. It was put in the basement, and along with the other remaining Chamber artifacts was eventually donated to the California Historical Society in 1984. In 1990 the collection became part of the University of Southern California's Regional History Center, which was located in a large building east of the campus. Curator Dace Taube put Frank out in the commodious Reading Room, happily informing everyone who asked, "Who's that?" But when the Center's staff moved to the Doheny Library, Frank had to stay behind. Now he surveys the Center's storage area. In the dark. *Sic transit gloria mundi*, L.A. style. 2007

ACKNOWLEDGMENTS

This book has been a very long time coming. My research began by studying with Anthony Turhollow at Loyola Marymount University and Norris Hundley at UCLA. Finding the remaining files at the Chamber of Commerce headquarters on Bixel while doing research for Theodore Saloutos at UCLA changed my topic of interest. My 1985 article on the promotion of Los Angeles for *California History* was urged on me by J.S. Holliday, the director of the California Historical Society. Tom Hines at UCLA was instrumental in helping me understand the importance of imagery in United States history.

Work on this book was helped by many people. Jim Beardsley, Ann Gray, Catherine Gudis, Roger Hathaway, Sister Margaret McKenna and Michael Sullivan all pushed the research along through their interest in the topic. Booksellers who share my fascination with Los Angeles were also helpful in discussing the topic and helping to find material—thanks to Michael Dawson, Andy Dowdy and Roger Gozdecki. Roger Hathaway not only shared his knowledge of L.A. history, but also his huge collection of ephemera, his talent and his patience for restoring damaged historical photographs. He risked his neck and the approbation of his wife and partner, Laura, by climbing up a windmill to get the contemporary oranges-and-snow photo on page 202. Paddy Calistro, Angel City Press publisher, loved the topic and always supported the book, while both she and Scott McAuley helped to improve the text. The incomparable Amy Inouye came up with the wonderful design—and never once ran screaming when I showed up with yet another handful of pictures.

Los Angeles is blessed to have two terrific women running the premier photo reserves in town. Carolyn Kozo Cole at the Los Angeles Public Library Collection and Dace Taube at the University of Southern California's Regional History Center know their collections intimately, and could not possibly have been more helpful. The same is true of Gary Kurutz at the State Library in Sacramento and Jennifer Watts at the Huntington. Ernie Marquez, whose L.A. roots go back to 1771, was generous in sharing his images of my hero, Frank Wiggins. Acknowledgment also must be made of those hundreds of eBay sellers who have found so many amazing images and made them available to collectors.

PHOTO CREDITS

All photographs and ephemera used in *Paradise Promoted* are from the Tom Zimmerman Collection, with the following exceptions:

Automobile Club of Southern California Archives: 116 top right, 151 right

California Bell Company (www.californiabell.com): 37 bottom right

California History Room, California State Library, Sacramento: 93 bottom, 138 bottom, 146 (pennant), 155 bottom center and right

California State University, Dominguez Hills: 147 right

Foster and Kleiser / Clear Channel Collection: 15, 17 top, 162

Friends of the Banning Residence Museum, Wilmington: 103 top center

Roger Hathaway: 202

Margaret Herrick Library / Academy of Motion Pictures Arts and Sciences: 126 top, 127 bottom

Library of Congress, Washington D.C.: 187 bottom right, 196 bottom right

Ernest Marquez Collection: 70 bottom left

Riverside Municipal Museum: 25

San Pedro Historical Society: 60 top left

Sierra Madre Historical Archives, Sierra Madre: 21

Seaver Center for Western History Research, Los Angeles County Museum of Natural History: 77 left

Security Pacific Collection / Los Angeles Public Library: 4, 39 top left, 47 right, 53 top right, 65, 67 top, 68 bottom, 70 top right, left and bottom right, 78, 90 right, 99 top left, 109 right, 117 top, 127 top, 142, 148 center right, 150 bottom, 155 top, 156, 163 bottom right, 168 top right, 195 top right

Sunkist Growers, Inc.: 24

University of Southern California Regional History Collection: 9, 41 top right, 76 center left and right, bottom right, 135 top, 144, 157 top right, 169 left

Tom Zimmerman Photography: 198, 199 top left, 200 bottom, 203

BIBLIOGRAPHIC ESSAY

The majority of the research for *Paradise Promoted* was done in the endless books and pamphlets that are the primary sources about the booster campaign. The earliest history of the promotional campaign is best found in the State Library in Sacramento, the Bancroft Library at U.C. Berkeley and at the glorious Huntington Library in San Marino. Southern California pamphlets can be found at UCLA Special Collections, Special Collections at Los Angeles Central Library, and in the Regional History Collection at USC. Excellent localized collections are at Santa Catalina Historical Collection, the Sierra Madre Library, and in the archives of California State University at Dominguez Hills. The vast majority of the Chamber of Commerce photographic collection is at the Los Angeles Central Library. Part of the Chamber photo collection, the Stenographer's Reports of the Board of Directors Meetings, Members' Annuals, pamphlets, prospectus books of the Industrial Bureau and a complete run of *Southern California Business* is at the Regional History Center at USC. The records and publications of the All Year Club are in the Urban Archives Center at California State University at Northridge. The entire promotional campaign can be tracked in the invaluable *Los Angeles Times* Historical Archive online through ProQuest and the Los Angeles Public Library.

The promotional campaign is discussed by Carey McWilliams in *Southern California: An Island on the Land* (New York: Sloan, Pearce, 1946); Kevin Starr, *Americans and the California Dream, 1850-1915* and *Material Dreams: Southern California Through the 1920s* (New York: Oxford University Press, 1973 and 1990); Stephanie Barron, Sheri Bernstein, Ilene Susan Fort, *Made in California: Art, Image, and Identity, 1900-2000* (Berkeley, Los Angeles: University of California Press, 2000). It is specifically covered by Richard Orsi, *Selling the Golden State: A Study of Boosterism in Nineteenth-Century California* (Dissertation, University of Wisconsin, 1973); Judith Elias, *Los Angeles: Dream to Reality, 1885-1915* (Northridge: Santa Susana Press, 1983); William McClung, *Landscapes of Desire: Anglo Mythologies of Los Angeles* (Berkeley, Los Angeles: University of California Press, 2000); K.D. and Gary Kurutz, *California Calls You: The Art of Promoting the Golden State, 1870-1940* (Sausalito: Windgate Press, 2000). For the history of the Chamber of Commerce see the work of Carolyn Kozo Cole, *Los Angeles Chamber of Commerce: From Agriculture to Aerospace* (Los Angeles: Chamber of Commerce, 1988); Charles Willard, *A History of the Chamber of Commerce of Los Angeles, California* (Los Angeles: Kingsley-Barnes & Neuner, 1899). For the use of photographs in the campaign, see Tom Zimmerman, "Paradise Promoted: Boosterism and the Los Angeles Chamber of Commerce," *California History*, 64 (Winter, 1985), 22-33; Jennifer Watts, "Picture Taking in Paradise" in Vanessa Schwartz,

Jeannene Pryzblyski, *The Nineteenth-Century Visual Culture Reader* (New York: Routledge, 2004) and "Photography in the Land of Sunshine," *Southern California Quarterly*, 87 (Winter 2005), 339-376. For a summation of the Chamber's view of its first six decades of work, see *The Sixty Year Progress of Los Angeles in Twenty-One Aspects* (Los Angeles: Chamber of Commerce, 1948).

CHAPTER 1: The earliest days of Los Angeles are admirably remembered by Harris Newmark, *Sixty Years in Southern California* (Los Angeles: Dawson's Book Shop, 1984). The permutations of the founding myth are followed by: Monsignor Francis Weber, *The Founding of Los Angeles: A Study in Historiography* (Los Angeles: Archdiocese Archives, 1970). The two best studies of the Ramona myth and the Southland are by George Wharton James, *Through Ramona's Country* (Boston: Little, Brown, 1909) and Dydia DeLyser, *Memories: Tourism and the Shaping of Southern California* (Minneapolis: University of Minnesota Press, 2005). For other chapter topics, see Ludwig Louis Salvator, *Los Angeles in the Sunny Seventies: A Flower in the Golden Land* (Los Angeles: Jake Zeitlin, 1929); Kate Sanborn, *A Truthful Woman in Southern California* (New York: D. Appleton, 1893); John Steven McGroarty, "When California Began," *San Gabriel Valley Monthly*, 1 (April, 1928), 5-6; Max Kurillo, Erline Tuttle, *California's El Camino Real and Its Historic Bells* (San Diego: Sunbelt, 2000). For a decidedly non-booster view of local natives, see Bernice Eastman Johnston, *California's Gabrielino Indians* (Los Angeles: Southwest Museum, 1964)

CHAPTER 2: The two key aspects of this chapter are covered admirably by Larry Mullaly and Bruce Petty, *The Southern Pacific in Los Angeles, 1873-1996* (San Marino: Golden West, 2002) and John Baur, *Health Seekers of Southern California* (San Marino: Huntington Library, 1959). For the two doctors' views, see William Edwards and Beatrice Harraden, *Two Health-Seekers in Southern California* (Philadelphia, 1897) and Peter Remondino, *The Mediterranean Shores of America* (Philadelphia, 1892). The railroads as promoters are specifically covered by Alfred Runte, "Promoting the Golden West: Advertising and the Railroad," *California History*, 70 (Spring, 1991), 62-75.

CHAPTER 3: For the Southland's favorite crop, see the work of Douglas Sackman, *Orange Empire: California and the Fruits of Eden* (Berkeley, Los Angeles: University of California Press, 2005. Sunkist is covered in *Heritage of Gold: The First 100 Years of Sunkist Growers, Inc., 1893-1993* (Los Angeles: Sunkist Growers, 1993). For Frank Wiggins' views on creating L.A. see his letter to the *New York Times*, July

3, 1920, 10. For Peter Clark MacFarlane's comments, see "The City That Advertising Built," *Collier's*, 55 (June 26, 1915), 11. Jane Meredith's letter is in the Giddings Archive, Pasadena.

CHAPTER 4: The boosters' view of the harbor is in John Steven McGroarty, *Los Angeles: A Maritime City* (Los Angeles: Chamber of Commerce, 1912). Other water matters are covered in Norris Hundley, Jr., *The Great Thirst: Californians and Water, 1770s-1990s* (Berkeley, Los Angeles: University of California Press, 1992). William Lacy's arguments for the Library are in *Stenographer's Report, Meeting of Board of Directors, Los Angeles Chamber of Commerce*, October 9, 1924, 1-11. Pride in the new industries is best expressed in: "Los Angeles the New Tire Center," *Southern California Business*, 6 (May, 1927), 9-10; A.B. Arnoll, "The Story of Industrial Growth is Fascinating," *Southern California Business*, 7 (January, 1929), 9-11; *Special Report to General Motors Corporation* (Los Angeles: Chamber of Commerce, 1929). For Willis Owen's comments, see *Knocking the Peak Off* (*Los Angeles Evening Express*, 1924).

CHAPTER 5: The best place to start reading about the Pacific Electric is still Spencer Crump, *Ride the Big Red Cars: How Trolleys Helped Build Southern California* (Corona del Mar: Trans-Anglo, 1970). Charles Seims, *Mt Lowe: The Trailway in the Clouds* (San Marino: Golden West, 1976) describes one mountain while John W. Robinson in *Sierra Madre's Old Mount Wilson Trail* (Sierra Madre: Big Santa Anita Historical Society, 2001) describes another. Henry Huntington's effect on the Southland is covered in William Friedricks, *Henry E. Huntington and the Creation of Southern California* (Columbus: Ohio State University Press, 1992). For the triumph of the auto, see Scott Bottles, *Los Angeles and the Automobile: The Making of the Modern City* (Berkeley, Los Angeles: University of California Press, 1987). A recommended video history of the P.E. is *This Was Pacific Electric* (Sky City Productions, 2003). For the history of the Auto Club, see the work of Kathy Talley-Jones, *The Road Ahead: The Automobile Club of Southern California, 1900- 2000* (Los Angeles: Automobile Club of Southern California, 2000). The history of Catalina is superbly covered by Richard and Marjorie Buffum, *Catalina Saga: An Historical Cruise Around Santa Catalina Island* (Balboa: Abracadabra Press, 2003).

CHAPTER 6: The general history of Hollywood is ably covered by Gregory Paul Williams, *The Story of Hollywood* (Los Angeles: BL Press, 2007). On the early film industry, see Eileen Bowser, *The Transformation of Cinema, 1907-1915* (New York: Charles Scribner's Sons, 1990); Kalton Lahue, *Motion Picture Pioneer: The Selig Polyscope Company* (New York: A.S. Barnes; 1973); Charles Clarke, *Early Film Making in Los Angeles* (Los Angeles: Dawson's Book Shop, 1976). For the ideas of two of the chief boosters of Hollywood see Cecil B. DeMille, "The Spotlight of Los Angeles," *Southern California Business*, 5 (July, 1926), 21; "Mary Pickford Says: Tree Planting Pays Big Dividends," *Southern California Business*, 6 (January, 1928), 14; Joseph Schenck, "A Business View of Motion Pictures," *Southern California Business*, 1 (June, 1922), 9. For the benefits of radio see Walter Fagan, "Making a New Conquest of the Air," *Southern California Business*, 8 (March, 1929), 20-21.

CHAPTER 7: For the aviation vision of pre-war L.A. see Aviation Committee, Los Angeles Chamber of Commerce, *A Comprehensive Report on the Master Plan of Airports* (Los Angeles: Los Angeles County Regional Planning District, 1940). Other topics in the chapter are discussed in Ford Carpenter, *The Land of the Beckoning Climate* (Los Angeles: Supervisors of Los Angeles County, 1941); William Garland, "Airplanes Will Take Land Values Up," *Los Angeles Realtor*, 6 (May, 1927), 11-12; A.W. Poole, "Where the Aviation Industry Centers," *Southern California Business*, 8 (May, 1929), 9-10; "Goodyear-Zeppelin Plant May Locate in Los Angeles," *Southern California Business*, 7 (February, 1928), 12-13; Edwin Clapp, "Los Angeles Should be the Home of Aircraft Industries," Reprinted from the *Los Angeles Examiner*, June 13, 1926 by the Los Angeles Chamber of Commerce.

CHAPTER 8: For the All Year Club, see C.G. Milham, "The All Year Club of Southern California," Western Advertising, 5 (April, 1923), 7-9; Frank Taylor, "Booster Number One," *Saturday Evening Post*, (April 4, 1942), 20-21. Other chapter topics are discussed in William C. DeMille, *Hollywood Saga* (New York: E.P. Dutton, 1939); Louis Adamic, "Los Angeles—Past and Present," *Haldeman-Julius Monthly*, (August, 1926), 39-47; Sarah Comstock, "The Great American Mirror: Reflections from Los Angeles," *Harper's Monthly*, 156 (May, 1928), 715-723; Farnsworth Crowder, "Los Angeles—the Heaven of Bunk-Shooters," *The Debunker and the American Parade*, 12 (June, 1930), 2-18. The early Chamber view of earthquakes is presented in *Los Angeles, May 1, 1906* (Los Angeles: Chamber of Commerce, 1906). A far less sanguine view is in Robert Hill, *Southern California Geology and Los Angeles Earthquakes* (Los Angeles: Southern California Academy of Sciences, 1928).

CHAPTER 9: For the business view of the Olympics see the words of William May Garland, "Mixing Games and Business Profitably," *Southern California Business*, 3 (December 1924), 15. For Los Angeles at war see Arthur Verge, *Paradise Transformed: Los Angeles During the Second World War* (Dubuque: Kendall/Hunt, 1993); Roger Butterfield, "Los Angeles is the Damndest Place . . . The City That Started with Nothing but Sunshine Now Expects to Become the Biggest in the World," *Life*, 15 (November 22, 1943), 102-104; "Los Angeles: The City Unlimited," *Business Week*, (August 10, 1946), 21-24. For the change in the view of L.A., see Tina Olsin Lent, "The Dark Side of the Dream: The Image of Los Angeles in Film Noir," and Linda Venis, "L.A. Novels and the Hollywood Dream Factory: Popular Art's Impact on Los Angeles Literature in the 1940s," *Southern California Quarterly*, 69 (Winter, 1987), 329-369.

INDEX

BE A BOOSTER---CALIFORNIA CATECHISM

Question—Where is the State of California located?
Answer—On the front side of the American continent, between the rest of the United States and the Pacific Ocean, and near the Panama canal.

Q.—Why is Southern California famous?
A.—It contains Los Angeles.

Q.—What is Los Angeles?
A.—The climatic capital of the United States.

Q.—To what has it been likened?
A.—To paradise, heaven, Eden and the Riviera.

Q.—Which does it most resemble?
A.—It is a happy combination of all of them.

Q.—What is the population of Los Angeles?
A.—700,000 boosters (Will be more tomorrow).

Q.—What is a booster?
A.—One who knows a good thing and wants others to come and share it.

Q.—Of whom does the population consist?
A.—Mostly of people from Iowa, together with many former residents of other states and a sprinkling of native sons.

Q.—Into what two classes may the people of the United States be divided?
A.—Those who have already seen Southern California and those who intend to see it soon.

Q.—What are Eastern visitors called while visiting Los Angeles? A.—Tourists.

Q.—What is a tourist?
A.—A permanent resident in the bud.

Q.—What things may a tourist see in and around Los Angeles that he does not see back East?
A.—Oranges, ostriches, lemons, alligators, olives, missions, sardines, aqueducts, harbors, tunas, bungalows, abalones, loquats, cassaba melons, horned toads, snow-covered peaks, submarine gardens, yuccas, eucalyptus, palms, pepper trees, cafeterias, Thanksgiving celery and Christmas strawberries.

Q.—Does L. A. hide its light under a bushel?
A.—It does not. In addition to showing the light it sets fire to the bushel and makes a conflagration that attracts the attention of the whole world.

Q.—Has L. A. any agents working for it in the East?
A.—Yes. Mr. Cyclone, Mr. Blizzard, Mr. Thunderstorm and the two Wave brothers, Messrs. Cold and Hot.

Q.—Are they successful?
A.—Highly so. They are sending thousands of people to Los Angeles every year.

Q.—When is the best time to come to Los Angeles?
A.—At once. "Everybody's doing it."

Q.—What is the only way to leave Los Angeles?
A.—With a return ticket.

Q.—When will Los Angeles cease to exceed the speed limit in growing? A.—When Gabriel blows his horn.

Q.—Where is the best place to eat in Los Angeles?
A.—BROADWAY CAFETERIA.

422 S. Broadway   Phone 614-51   Los Angeles